PENGUIN  CLASSICS

GORGIAS

PLATO (c. 427–347 B.C.) stands with Socrates and Aristotle as one of the shapers of the whole intellectual tradition of the West. He came from a family that had long played a prominent part in Athenian politics, and it would have been natural for him to follow the same course. He declined to do so however, disgusted by the violence and corruption of Athenian political life, and sickened especially by the execution in 399 of his friend and teacher, Socrates. Inspired by Socrates' inquiries into the nature of ethical standards, Plato sought a cure for the ills of society not in politics but in philosophy, and arrived at his fundamental and lasting conviction that those ills would never cease until philosophers became rulers or rulers philosophers. At an uncertain date in the early fourth century B.C. he founded in Athens the Academy, the first permanent institution devoted to philosophical research and teaching, and the prototype of all western universities. He travelled extensively, notably in Sicily as political adviser to Dionysius II, ruler of Syracuse.

Plato wrote over twenty philosophical dialogues, and here are also extant under his name thirteen letters, whose genuineness is keenly disputed. His literary activity extended over perhaps half a century: few other writers have exploited so effectively the grace and precision, the flexibility and power, of Greek prose.

WALTER HAMILTON was Master of Magdalen College, Cambridge, from 1967 to 1978 and is now an Honorary Fellow. He was born in 1908 and was a Scholar of Trinity College, Cambridge, where he gained first class honours in both parts of the classical Tripos. He was a Fellow of Trinity College and a University Lecturer at Cambridge, and taught at Eton before becoming Headmaster of Westminster School (1950–57) and of Rugby School (1957–66). He has translated Ammianus Marcellinus's *The Later Roman Empire* and Plato's *Symposium* and his *Phaedrus and Letters VII and VIII* for the Penguin Classics.

PLATO

GORGIAS

TRANSLATED
WITH AN INTRODUCTION BY
WALTER HAMILTON

PENGUIN BOOKS

Penguin Books Ltd, Harmondsworth, Middlesex, England
Viking Penguin Inc., 40 West 23rd Street, New York, New York 10010, U.S.A.
Penguin Books Australia Ltd, Ringwood, Victoria, Australia
Penguin Books Canada Limited, 2801 John Street, Markham, Ontario, Canada L3R 1B4
Penguin Books (N.Z.) Ltd, 182–190 Wairau Road, Auckland 10, New Zealand

—

This translation first published 1960
Reprinted with revisions 1971
Reprinted 1973, 1975, 1976, 1977, 1979, 1980, 1981,
1982, 1983, 1985, 1986, 1987

—

—

Made and printed in Great Britain by
Hazell Watson & Viney Limited,
Member of the BPCC Group,
Aylesbury, Bucks
Set in Monotype Garamond

CONTENTS

INTRODUCTION

I

THE GORGIAS has as a sub-title in some manuscripts the words 'Concerning oratory'. Gorgias himself is a professor of oratory, and the dialogue opens with a discussion between him and Socrates on the nature of his art. It soon becomes clear, however, that the true concern of the *Gorgias* is with ethics, and its scope cannot be better indicated than by a quotation from Socrates' concluding words: 'All the other theories put forward in our long conversation have been refuted, and this conclusion alone stands firm, that one should avoid wrong-doing with more care than being wronged, and that the supreme object of a man's efforts, in public and private life, must be the reality rather than the appearance of goodness.' The dialogue is in fact a passionate defence by Socrates of the ideal for which he gave his life, that man's business on earth is to discover and do what is right, and if we ask what this ideal has to do with oratory the answer is that in Plato's view it stands in direct opposition to the ends which the oratorical training of his day was adapted to serve.

To us the ability to speak acceptably and convincingly in public is a relatively trivial factor in the ordinary citizen's equipment for a successful life; to the ambitious Athenian of the fifth and fourth centuries B.C. it was essential. In the small but highly-developed democracy of which he was a member, participation by all the citizens in politics was taken for granted; the most important issues were settled by a debate of the whole citizen body; and the method of lot which governed the appointment of many officials might at any time place an individual in a position of great, if temporary, prominence. Moreover, in a community which was intensely litigious and in which representation by professional advocates was unknown, a man's property or even his life might depend on his power to sway a large court of his fellow-citizens, always more open to emotion than to logic. In these circumstances it is not surprising that the itinerant popular educators known as Sophists should have found among the young men of the Athenian upper classes an audience eager to pay high fees for lessons in oratory, and that those who professed to be able to impart its secrets claimed, like Gorgias, that the subject of their art was 'the greatest and best of human concerns'. On the other hand, the dangers of such an accomplishment in the hands of the ignorant or unscrupulous were sufficiently obvious then as now – the new-fangled art which can make the worse cause appear the better was scathingly satirized in 423 B.C. by Aristophanes in the *Clouds* – and Plato saw in it the breeding-ground of all that was false and corrupt in the life of his time. So it is that the discussion of the nature of rhetoric or oratory at the beginning of the *Gorgias* leads by a natural transition to a discussion of its immoral implications, and it is against the background sketched in this paragraph that the contrast between the true philosopher and the product of rhetorical training is to be studied, a contrast embodied in the persons of Socrates and Callicles.

II

The setting of the dialogue is of the simplest kind, and, if we except Chaerophon, whose part is negligible, the persons engaged in it number only four, Socrates himself, Gorgias, Polus, and Callicles. The scene is vague; Socrates encounters the others apparently in the open air at a moment when Gorgias, a distinguished visitor in Athens, has just given a public exhibition of his oratorical skill. Socrates expresses a wish to discuss with Gorgias the nature of his art, and is invited by Callicles, Gorgias' host, to come to his house for the purpose. Whether a change of scene is to be assumed at this point we are not told; without further preliminaries we are launched on the main business of the dialogue, the structure of which is as simple as its setting. There is little or no general conversation; Socrates converses with each of the other participants in turn, and the argument falls into three corresponding phases, marked by an increasingly earnest and vehement

tone as the issues at stake become clearer and more fundamental. Gorgias, a native of Leontini in Sicily, who came
to Athens in 427 B.C. with other delegates to ask for aid
for his city against Syracuse, is a man of considerable age
and international reputation as an orator and teacher of
oratory, and, though there is something faintly absurd in
the complacency of his earlier answers, he is treated by
Socrates with genuine respect. He is indeed a thoroughly
respectable man. Though he is known from other sources
to have been completely sceptical in metaphysics, he does
not carry this scepticism into the sphere of ethics. He
claims that the accomplished orator will need no other
specialized knowledge of any kind to get the better of
expert opposition on any subject, but he shrinks from
extending this claim to moral questions, and, though he
has earlier asserted that a teacher of oratory has no respon-
sibility for the use to which a pupil puts his teaching, he
admits in the end that he would feel bound to give instruction in morals to a pupil who needed it, before putting into
his hands the weapon of oratory. For all his reputation as
an intellectual giant of the new age, Gorgias turns out to
be a conventional person, and at this stage he is replaced
in the conversation by his younger colleague and admirer,
Polus, who proclaims his readiness to break with the
orthodox morality to which his master still pays allegiance.

Polus, like Gorgias, is an historical character and a native
of Sicily, of whom, however, we know little except that
he was the author of a treatise on oratory, of which his
sententious and mannered reply to Chaerophon on page 21
is presumably a sample, if it is not a parody. Whatever may
have been his real character he is represented by Plato as
living up to his name of Polus or 'Colt'; the impetuous
self-confidence with which at the beginning of the dialogue
he tries to take its whole burden on himself is matched
only by his incompetence at the Socratic method of argument, and Socrates treats him with a humorous conde-
scension which contrasts strongly with his attitude towards
Gorgias. Polus' demand that Socrates should himself define
the nature of oratory opens the way for the unsparing
attack upon contemporary politicians which is one of the
most noticeable features of the *Gorgias*. Oratory, we are

told, has no more claim to be a genuine art than cookery; both aim at the immediate gratification of the consumer without any regard for his welfare or any attempt to proceed on rational principles, and there is nothing to be envied in the so-called power of the successful speaker, since its results are often as fatal to the real interests of its possessor as to those on whom it is exercised.

To this Polus' answer is simply to charge Socrates with hypocrisy. Whatever he may profess he would certainly change places with a dictator, however criminal, if he had the chance. Socrates replies that he would not, and proceeds to enunciate the ethical doctrine which is the core of the whole dialogue, that 'it is better to suffer wrong than to do wrong'. Polus treats this at first as an absurd paradox, and it is unnecessary to summarize the arguments by which he is driven to admit its truth. What emerges is that in spite of his bold talk Polus is as much hampered by conventional scruples as Gorgias. He cannot bring himself to deny that doing wrong is an 'uglier' or 'baser' thing than suffering wrong, and this leads to his downfall. The second 'act' of the *Gorgias* closes with the triumphant establishment by Socrates not only of his main principle, but also of the corollary that not to be punished for his faults is the worst fate that can befall a wrong-doer.

The stage is now set for the entrance of Callicles, who has listened with growing impatience to the victory of what he regards as preposterous nonsense. His attitude is very much what we might expect in our own day from a convinced believer in power politics confronted by a proposal that the principles of the Sermon on the Mount should be universally adopted in their literal sense. For him conventional morality is simply a device invented by the weak as a defence against the strong, who are their natural superiors (the contrast of *nomos* and *physis*, law and nature, was one of the sophistic commonplaces of the age), and the only morality worthy of a man is the morality of 'might is right'.[1]

1. The view that moral standards are purely conventional and that the strong man is entitled to violate them if he can do so with impunity has had a long and influential subsequent history. (It is, for example, in essence the view of Nietzsche and is used by Raskolnikov to justify his crime in Dostoyevsky's *Crime and Punishment*.)

His ideal is the complete antithesis of that represented by
Socrates, who recognizes at once that he has to deal with
an opponent of very different calibre from Gorgias and
Polus, and it is in the clash between these two ideals in
their extremest form that the chief interest of the dialogue
consists.

Nothing is otherwise known of Callicles, and it has
generally been supposed that he is a fictitious personage,
invented by Plato to embody the principles which he so
strongly maintains. Against this it may be argued that the
mention of his deme of Acharnae (p. 96) gives an impres-
sion of fact, and, more convincingly, that it is not Plato's
habit to introduce imaginary characters as direct participants in a dialogue. The question must remain open; but,
whether fictitious or not, Callicles, who is young, rich, and
ambitious, represents a type of which Athenian history in
the closing years of the fifth century furnished a number of
of instances. Several were to be found among the Thirty
Tyrants, a ruthless oligarchy which seized power after Athens'
final defeat in the Peloponnesian War, but the supreme
example is perhaps Alcibiades. It is worth recalling that it
was under his influence that Athens in 416 B.C. demanded
the surrender of the small and unoffending island of Melos,
and on its refusal killed its men and enslaved its other
inhabitants. Thucydides has made the episode the occasion
for a dialogue between Athenians and Melians, in which
the former frankly assert that it is the law of nature that
the stronger should rule over the weaker – 'the strong exact
what they can and the weak submit' – and no better illustration could be found of the philosophy of Callicles in
action, though modern history presents us with many on
a larger scale.

It is important to recognize that the life for which
Callicles invites Socrates to abandon philosophy is a life

I call it sophistic because the distinction between natural right and
man-made law and custom is first found in several of the Sophists,
who were predominantly sceptical of traditional standards. In the
extreme form expounded by Callicles it occurs in a fragment of the
Sophist Antiphon. For Sophists in general, cf. Plato's *Protagoras*
and W. K. C. Guthrie's introduction to his Penguin translation of
that dialogue.

of strenuous activity. His super-man will encourage his passions to be as violent as possible and stop at nothing in order to gratify them, but Callicles is no vulgar hedonist, and, although he begins by identifying good with pleasure, he recoils with disgust from the conclusion that the most depraved sensualist, provided that he can secure the satisfaction of his desires, will come as near to fulfilling his ideal as the successful man of action. In the end he is forced to admit a distinction between good and bad pleasures, and this distinction enables Socrates to return once more to his condemnation of contemporary politicians for ministering to the pleasure rather than the welfare of their hearers, and ultimately to enunciate again his fundamental principle that correction is better for those who suffer it, be they individuals or states, than the complete absence of restraint which Callicles extols as the ideal.

Callicles' disgust at this outcome is such that from this point he refuses to give any but formal answers to the questions put to him, and what remains is virtually a monologue by Socrates, in which the choice between philosophy and a public life is examined in the light of the conclusions already established. It may well be that Callicles is right in his contention that the philosopher will be at the mercy of anyone who chooses to injure or even to kill him, but immunity from injury or death is not worth purchasing at the expense of lowering oneself to the standards of the ruling power, in this case the Athenian democracy, and thus being involved in the admittedly greater evil of wrongdoing. Moreover, in view of the distinction that has been drawn between the genuine arts like medicine or the administration of justice, which employ a basis of knowledge to secure the welfare of their objects, and the pseudo-arts like cookery or oratory which aim simply at giving pleasure, it is clear that a man will be justified in embarking on a political career only if he possesses a knowledge of moral values which will enable him to improve the character of the community. Judged by this criterion the most eminent Athenian statesmen, including Pericles, fail miserably: good ministers to the desires of the public they may have been, but nothing more, and Socrates refuses to join the ranks of those whom he has rudely but emphatically called 'panders'. He makes, in fact, what to his audience must seem the amazing claim that he himself, by making it his constant object to improve rather than to please his hearers, is perhaps the only living man who deserves the name of statesman, and he ends by asserting that if his persistence in this course leads him to his death, which is what he expects, he will be prepared to meet it with serenity.

Finally, to reinforce the conclusion that wrong-doing is the worst misfortune that can befall a man, Socrates gives an account of judgement after death, cast in the form of a myth, though he himself professes to regard it as the truth. This is not the place for a discussion of Platonic myths in general; it must suffice to say that Plato employs the poetic form of myth to convey his beliefs on topics to which the rigidly logical process of dialectic is not applicable, and one such topic is the fate of the soul in the next world. That the details of such eschatological myths are not meant to be literally interpreted is made plain by the comment attached to the similar myth in the *Phaedo*, where Socrates remarks that no sensible man would insist upon the strict accuracy of such a picture of the world to come as he has just drawn, but that to believe that this or something like it is true is a risk worth taking. In any case, here as in the *Republic* with its corresponding myth of Er, it has already been proved that, irrespective of consequences, it is better to suffer wrong than to do wrong.

III

The scope of the *Gorgias* has been indicated in barest outline; it remains to consider its place in the context of Plato's life and thought as a whole. First, however, a word about the dramatic date of the dialogue may not be out of place. The internal evidence for this is confusing and inconsistent; the time is as vague as the rest of the setting. On p. 61 Socrates speaks of having presided over the Assembly 'last year'. It is generally held that this is an ironically modest reference to his behaviour on the only occasion on which he is known to have presided, when at the trial of the commanders after the naval battle of Arginusae in

406 B.C. he refused in the face of intense popular clamour to put to the vote a motion that all the accused should be tried together. If this assumption is right – and it is difficult to suppose that if Socrates had presided on another occasion we should nowhere be told of it – the dramatic date of the dialogue would appear to be securely fixed in 405, and this is consistent with the references to Archelaus of Macedonia, who came to power about 413. On the other hand Gorgias, who appears to be on his first visit to Athens, was certainly there in 427; Pericles, who died in 429, is spoken of as 'lately dead'; Nicias and Aristocrates, who died in 413 and 406 respectively, the former in the Sicilian catastrophe and the latter actually as one of the condemned Arginusae commanders, are referred to as distinguished living figures; Demos, the son of Pyrilampes, the object of Callicles' passion, is mentioned by Aristophanes as a celebrated beauty in the *Wasps* of 422. In the face of these conflicting pieces of evidence we can only fall back on more general considerations, and these are decisively in favour of a date towards the end of Socrates' life. He is an established and mature thinker, who treats the famous Gorgias as an equal and Polus expressly as a much younger man, and the warnings which Callicles repeatedly utters of the fate which is likely to overtake him if he persists in his present course, and Socrates' own acceptance of the likelihood, would be singularly out of place if he were not already far advanced in the philosophic mission which led to his execution. The only sound conclusion is to accept 405 or something like it as the period at which the conversation is supposed to have taken place, and to recognize that Plato, who is notoriously careless of anachronisms, has been unusually so in the present dialogue.

It is of more interest and importance to consider where the *Gorgias* stands in the history of Plato's development, and here, though we have no external evidence, all the indications point to the earlier years of his literary career. The complete absence of metaphysics, and in particular of the doctrines generally recognized as distinctively Platonic, is enough by itself to make this conclusion practically certain, and in this connexion a comparison with the *Republic* is especially instructive. Fundamentally the theme of both dialogues is the same, a demonstration that the life of the just man is intrinsically preferable to the life of the unjust, whatever the external circumstances of either. Thrasymachus in the first book of the *Republic* with his thesis that right consists in the interest of the stronger is simply Callicles under another name, and the claim put forward by Socrates in the *Gorgias* that he is the only genuine living statesman finds its counterpart in the *Republic* in the monopoly of power reserved for philosopher-kings. But the conclusions of the *Republic*, though ethically identical with those of the *Gorgias*, are infinitely more complex, based as they are on the metaphysics of the Theory of Ideas as well as on an elaborate psychology, and it is inconceivable that either can have been formulated in Plato's mind at the time when he composed the *Gorgias*. It follows with certainty that the *Gorgias* is to be assigned to a period earlier not only than the *Republic* but also than any other dialogue, such as the *Phaedo* or *Symposium*, which involves the Theory of Ideas in anything like a fully developed form.

We may indeed with considerable plausibility go further. Readers of the *Gorgias* cannot fail to be struck by the peculiar bitterness and intolerance of its tone towards politics and politicians, so unlike the urbanity which Socrates is usually represented as exhibiting towards his opponents. It reads like the work of an angry man, or at least of a man labouring under very strong emotion, and we know from Plato's own fragment of autobiography in the *Seventh Letter* that his state of mind after the death of Socrates in 399 was precisely that which the dialogue reveals. He was then twenty-eight, and the hopes of a political career which he had once entertained were dead. They had begun to wither five years earlier when his innocent expectation of a period of pure rule under the oligarchy of the Thirty, some of whom were his friends and relatives, quickly turned to horror at the wickedness of their proceedings, and, though he had again contemplated entering politics at the restoration of the democracy in 403, his disillusion became complete and permanent when the restored democrats condemned and executed Socrates. He then came to the conclusion, he tells us, that all existing forms of government were bad, and that philosophy held the only hope for the salvation of society; in fact, that the crimes and miseries of mankind would have no end until either philosophers attained political power or those with political power became philosophers.[1] Not only may we reasonably conclude that the *Gorgias* with its unusual intemperance of tone is a product of the period when Plato's own feelings on politics were at their most bitter; it is surely not fanciful to find in Callicles' scorn of philosophy, and in the reproaches with which he loads Socrates for neglecting the proper use of his natural gifts and clinging as a mature man to a pursuit which he should have left behind with his boyhood, echoes of the kind of language which must have been used to Plato himself by his relations and early associates when he announced his intention of abandoning for ever what in his position and with his endowments were exceptionally brilliant prospects of a political career.

It may be asked why, in the absence from the *Gorgias* of any specifically Platonic doctrine, we should hesitate to take the dialogue at its face value as a record of the opinions of the historical Socrates. How much in the earlier dialogues of Plato is to be regarded as Socratic is a problem on which dogmatism is to be avoided, but if the view put forward in the last paragraph is accepted, that the *Gorgias* is to a large extent inspired by Plato's own experience, the question is already answered, at least in part. In any case the opinion has generally prevailed among scholars that Socrates, who wrote nothing, confined himself to a search for general definitions of moral concepts, and that in positive doctrine he did not go beyond the enunciation of such paradoxes as 'virtue is knowledge' and 'no one willingly does wrong'. It would therefore be dangerous to attribute to him such elaborate arguments as that, for example, by which pleasure is distinguished from good in the *Gorgias*, still more the solemn and almost prophetic warning of judgement to come with which the dialogue closes – it is

1. For this letter cf. W. Hamilton's translation of Plato: *Phaedrus* and *The Seventh and Eighth Letters* (Penguin Classics), pp. 111 *ff*. Cf. also H. D. P. Lee's introduction to his translation of the *Republic* (Penguin Classics), pp.13 *ff*.

noteworthy that in the *Apology* he does not commit himself on the subject of the soul's survival after death; he is simply confident that no harm can happen to a good man. Nevertheless, the *Gorgias* is built around a central paradox of the simplest kind, which is eminently consistent both in tone and content with what is normally accepted as Socratic, the paradox that 'it is better to suffer wrong than to do wrong', and the present translator sees nothing improbable in the supposition that this was one of the actual pronouncements of Socrates.

It would be foolish to claim for the *Gorgias* a place in the very front rank among the Platonic dialogues. Some of its detailed argument is prolix and unconvincing, and, though the characters of Polus and Callicles are revealed with a skill and economy of which only Plato is capable, no attempt is made to conciliate the reader's interest by the creation of an elaborate setting such as constitutes the main charm of the *Protagoras*. But, though it cannot challenge comparison with the profundity and richness of thought of the *Republic*, still less with the miraculous combination of philosophic depth and artistic perfection exhibited by the *Symposium*, the *Gorgias* by its very directness and lack of adornment creates an effect which is immensely impressive. The conflict of principles which it depicts with unsurpassed clarity and moving eloquence is a conflict which is perennial both for communities and for individuals; it will not escape notice that the ideal of Callicles is the ideal of Nietzsche and Carlyle, or that the proposition which Socrates opposes to it lies at the heart of Christian, no less than of Platonic, ethics. As long as the forces of goodness and expediency continue their struggle for men's allegiance the *Gorgias* is secure of its place among the great masterpieces of ethical literature.

W.H.

Ardbeg, Isle of Mull

GORGIAS

CALLICLES. Your arrival, Socrates, is the kind they 447 recommend for a war or a battle.

SOCRATES. Do you imply that, in the proverbial phrase, we are late for a feast?[1]

CALLICLES. You are indeed, and a very fine feast too. Gorgias has just finished displaying all manner of lovely things to us.

SOCRATES. It is Chaerephon who is to blame for this, Callicles; he made us linger in the market-place.

CHAEREPHON. Never mind, Socrates, I'll put the matter right. Gorgias is a friend of mine and will give us a demonstration, now, if you like, or, if you prefer, at some other time.

CALLICLES. Does Socrates really want to hear Gorgias, Chaerephon?

CHAEREPHON. That is exactly what we are here for.

CALLICLES. Then you can gratify your desire by coming home with me. Gorgias is staying with me, and will, I am sure, put on a demonstration for you.

SOCRATES. Splendid, Callicles, but would he be willing to enter into conversation with us? I want to ask him what the power of his art consists in and what it is that he professes and teaches. The demonstration can wait for some other time, as you say.

CALLICLES. There is nothing like asking himself, Socrates. As a matter of fact, one of the features of his demonstration just now was an invitation to any one in the house to ask what questions he liked, accompanied by a promise to answer them all.

1. Whatever the exact form of the proverb here referred to, the general sense must be 'first at a feast, last at a fight'. The Neo-Platonic commentator Olympiodorus tells us that Gorgias excited such enthusiasm at Athens that the days on which he lectured were called 'feast-days'.

SOCRATES. Excellent news. Ask him, Chaerephon.

CHAEREPHON. Ask him what?

SOCRATES. What sort of man he is.

CHAEREPHON. What do you mean?

SOCRATES. Well, if he happened to be a manufacturer of shoes, for example, he would presumably answer that he was a shoemaker. Now do you understand?

CHAEREPHON. Perfectly. I'll ask him. Tell me, Gorgias, is Callicles speaking the truth when he says that you offer to answer any question that is put to you?

448 GORGIAS. Yes, Chaerephon. That is precisely the offer which I made just now, and I may say that no one has put a new question to me for many years.

CHAEREPHON. Then you will have no difficulty in answering, Gorgias.

GORGIAS. Try and see, Chaerephon.

POLUS. Try by all means; but let me be the object of your experiment, if you don't mind, Chaerephon. Gorgias is worn out, I'm sure, after all that he has just been through.

CHAEREPHON. How is this, Polus? Do you suppose that you could answer better than Gorgias?

POLUS. What difference does that make, provided that my answer satisfies you?

CHAEREPHON. No difference at all. Do the answering by all means, if you like.

POLUS. Put your question.

CHAEREPHON. Here it is, then. If Gorgias were an expert in the same art as his brother Herodicus, what would be the right name to give him? The same as his brother, presumably?

POLUS. Of course.

CHAEREPHON. Then we should be right to call him a doctor?

POLUS. Yes.

CHAEREPHON. But if his art were the same as that of Aristophon, the son of Aglaophon, or *his* brother,[1] what should we be right to call him then?

POLUS. A painter, obviously.

CHAEREPHON. Well then, what is the art in which Gorgias is expert, and what would be the corresponding right name to give him?

POLUS. There are a number of arts, Chaerephon, which men have discovered empirically as a result of experience; for it is experience that enables us to organize our lives systematically, whereas lack of experience leaves us at the mercy of chance. Different men practise different arts in different ways, but the best men practise the best arts. Gorgias is one of these, and the art which he practises is the finest of them all.[2]

SOCRATES. I see, Gorgias, that Polus is endowed with a splendid gift of eloquence, but he isn't doing what he promised Chaerephon.

GORGIAS. What do you mean exactly, Socrates?

SOCRATES. As far as I can see, he is simply not answering the question.

GORGIAS. Put it to him yourself then, if you like.

SOCRATES. Not if you would consent to answer it personally; I would much rather put it to you. From what he has said it is clear to me that Polus has devoted himself much more to what is called oratory than to the art of conversation.

POLUS. Why do you say that, Socrates?

SOCRATES. Because, when Chaerephon asks you what art Gorgias is master of, you embark on a panegyric

1. This curiously oblique description conceals the name of Polygnotus, one of the most celebrated of all Greek painters.

2. This speech is probably a quotation from Polus' own treatise on oratory (cf. p. 43 and Introduction, p. 9). It is a specimen of the mannered antithetical style introduced by Gorgias, and no doubt exaggerated by his uncritical admirer Polus.

of his art as if some one were attacking it, without, however, saying what it is.

POLUS. Didn't I say that it was the finest of the arts?

SOCRATES. Certainly. But what you were asked was not how you would describe Gorgias' art but what it is and what Gorgias should be called. Just answer these questions in the same excellent and concise way as you did the questions which Chaerephon put to you at first by way of examples. Or better still, tell us yourself, Gorgias, what your art is and what in consequence we ought to call you.

GORGIAS. My art is oratory, Socrates.

SOCRATES. Then we ought to call you an orator?[1]

GORGIAS. Yes, and a good orator, if you want to call me what, in Homer's phrase, 'I boast myself to be'.

SOCRATES. That is exactly what I do want.

GORGIAS. Then call me that.

SOCRATES. Now are we to say that you can make others what you are yourself?

GORGIAS. That is precisely what I profess to do at Athens and elsewhere.

SOCRATES. Would you be willing then, Gorgias, to continue the discussion on the present lines, by way of question and answer, and to put off to another occasion the kind of long continuous discourse that Polus was embarking on? Be true to your promise, and show yourself willing to give brief answers to what you are asked.

GORGIAS. Some answers, Socrates, necessarily require a speech of some length. But all the same I will try to be as brief as possible. As a matter of fact one of the claims I make is that nobody can express a given idea more concisely than I.

SOCRATES. Just what is needed, Gorgias. Give me

1. The word *rhetor*, here and elsewhere translated 'orator', has the double sense of 'orator' and 'teacher of oratory'.

a demonstration of your talent for brevity and let the opposite wait for another occasion.

GORGIAS. Very well; I'll force you to admit that you have never heard anyone more concise.

SOCRATES. Come then: you say that you understand the art of oratory and can make orators of others. What is the object with which oratory is concerned? Weaving for example is concerned with the production of clothes, is it not?

GORGIAS. Yes.

SOCRATES. And music with the creation of melodies?

GORGIAS. Yes.

SOCRATES. My word, Gorgias, your answers are an absolute miracle of brevity, I must say.

GORGIAS. Yes, I think I'm pretty good at brevity, Socrates.

SOCRATES. You are indeed. Well, answer now in the same way abour oratory. What is it that oratory is the knowledge of?

GORGIAS. Speech.

SOCRATES. What sort of speech, Gorgias? The kind which tells the sick how they must live in order to get well?

GORGIAS. No.

SOCRATES. Then oratory is not concerned with every kind of speech?

GORGIAS. Certainly not.

SOCRATES. But you would say that it makes men good at speaking?

GORGIAS. Yes.

SOCRATES. And presumably good at thinking about the subjects on which it teaches them to speak?

GORGIAS. Of course.

SOCRATES. Now, does medicine, which we mentioned just now, make men good at thinking and speaking about the sick? 450

GORGIAS. Necessarily.

SOCRATES. So it appears that medicine too is concerned with speech?

GORGIAS. Yes.

SOCRATES. Speech about ailments?

GORGIAS. Of course.

SOCRATES. Similarly, physical training is concerned with speech about the fitness of our bodies and the opposite?

GORGIAS. Undoubtedly.

SOCRATES. And the same is true about all the other arts, Gorgias. Each of them is concerned with the kind of speech that is relevant to the subject with which each art deals.

GORGIAS. So it seems.

SOCRATES. Then, since you call whatever art is concerned with speech oratory, why do you not call the other arts oratory, seeing that they are admittedly concerned with speech?

GORGIAS. Because, Socrates, whereas with the other arts the knowledge appropriate to them is almost wholly concerned with manual operations and such like, there is nothing analogous in the case of oratory, which does its work and produces its effect entirely by means of speech. That is why I assert that the art of oratory is the art of speech *par excellence*, and I maintain that I am right.

SOCRATES. I am not sure that I understand what sort of character you mean to give to oratory, but I shall know more clearly by and by. Tell me – we recognize the existence of arts, do we not?

GORGIAS. Yes.

SOCRATES. Now among all the arts there are, I think, some which consist mainly of action and have little or no need of speech, arts such as painting and sculpture and many others, whose business could be carried on in positive silence. It is with arts such as these, I suppose, that you say that oratory has no concern. Am I right?

GORGIAS. Absolutely right, Socrates.

SOCRATES. But there are other arts which achieve their whole effect by speech, and have no need of action – or very little – arithmetic, for example, and calculation[1] and geometry and I would add games like backgammon and so on. In some of them speech and action play almost equal parts, but in many speech is the more important and is entirely responsible for the whole business and its result. It is in this class that you place oratory, I think?

GORGIAS. Certainly.

SOCRATES. But I don't believe that you really mean to call any of these arts oratory, though anybody who took at its face value your assertion that oratory is the art which achieves its effects by means of speech might, if he were disposed to quibble, come to the conclusion that arithmetic is oratory in your view, Gorgias. All the same I don't suppose that you would call either arithmetic or geometry oratory.

GORGIAS. You are quite right not to suppose so, Socrates. 451

SOCRATES. Well then, finish your answer to the question which I was asking you. If oratory is one of those arts which chiefly employ speech and there are other arts in the same class, try to say what is the subject about which oratory achieves its effects in speech. If anyone were to ask me about one of the arts which I mentioned just now, 'Tell me, Socrates, what is the art of arithmetic?' I should reply, just as you did, that it is one of the arts which achieves its results by means of speech. And if he were to go on

1. Greek distinguishes between *arithmetic*, the theory of numbers, and *calculation*, the practical art of reckoning. For the purpose of this argument, speech and writing are not distinguished; both may be regarded as forms of speech.

to ask 'Speech about what?' I should say about odd
and even numbers of whatever magnitude. If he
were then to ask 'What do you mean by the art of
calculation?', I should answer that this too is one
of the class which does its whole business by means
of speech. And if he proceeded to ask its subject, I
should say, like those who draft amendments for the
assembly,[1] that except in one point what we have
said of arithmetic may stand, calculation and arithmetic both being concerned with the same subject,
odd and even; calculation, however, contemplates
the magnitude of odd and even numbers relatively
to one another as well as absolutely. And if in reply
to a question about astronomy I said that this too
does its whole work by means of speech, and were
then asked 'Speech about what, Socrates?', I should
reply, 'About the movements of the stars and the
sun and the moon and their relative speeds'.

GORGIAS. A very good answer, Socrates.

SOCRATES. Then follow my example, Gorgias. Isn't
oratory one of those arts which exclusively employ
speech for the accomplishment of their work and
purpose?

GORGIAS. It is.

SOCRATES. Then tell me its subject. What thing is it
that forms the subject of all the speech that oratory
employs?

GORGIAS. The greatest and best of human concerns,
Socrates.

SOCRATES. But even this answer, Gorgias, is open to
dispute and far from clear. You have heard, I suppose, people at parties singing the well-known song
which enumerates man's blessings and asserts that

1. The reference is to some stereotyped official formula for
framing additions or amendments to motions brought before
the Assembly by the Council, e.g. 'For x read y; the rest stands
as in the original text'.

the greatest blessing is health, the next beauty, and the third, according to the author of the song, wealth honestly come by?[1]

GORGIAS. Of course I have heard it. But how is it relevant here?

SOCRATES. Because your answer will at once bring down upon you the producers of the blessings praised by the author of the song, the doctor and the trainer and the man of business. Take the doctor first. 'Gorgias is deceiving you, Socrates,' he will say; 'it is my art, not his, that deals with man's chief blessing.' If I ask him who he is to talk like this, he will answer, I suppose, that he is a doctor. 'What do you mean then? Is the product of your art the greatest blessing?' 'How can it be otherwise, Socrates,' he will say, 'seeing that it is health? What greater blessing can a man possess than health?'

Suppose next that the trainer were to say: 'I should be surprised, Socrates, if Gorgias could demonstrate that the product of his art is a greater blessing than the product of mine.' I should say to him, as I did to the doctor: 'Who are you, my good man, and what is your job?' 'I am a trainer,' he would say, 'and my job is to make men physically beautiful and strong.'

After the trainer would come the man of business, I suppose, filled with a fine contempt for every other class. 'Do you really think, Socrates, that a greater blessing than wealth is to be found either with Gorgias or with anyone else?' 'What?' we should say to him, 'are you the man who produces wealth?' 'Yes.' 'In what capacity?' 'As a man of business.' 'Well,' we should say, 'do you think that wealth is the greatest of human blessings?' 'Of course.' 'And yet', we should go on, 'here is Gorgias who main-

452

---

1. Plato refers to this particular *scolion* or drinking-song in several other dialogues. Later writers attribute its authorship to Simonides or Epicharmus.

tains that the art which he possesses is productive of a greater blessing than yours.' Obviously he would ask next: 'What is this blessing? Let Gorgias answer.'

So then, Gorgias, imagine that you are being asked this question by these men as well as by me, and tell us what it is that you declare to be the greatest blessing man can enjoy and that you claim to be able to produce.

GORGIAS. I mean, Socrates, what is in actual truth the greatest blessing, which confers on every one who possesses it not only freedom for himself but also the power of ruling his fellow-countrymen.

SOCRATES. What do you mean by that?

GORGIAS. I mean the ability to convince by means of speech a jury in a court of justice, members of the Council in their Chamber, voters at a meeting of the Assembly, and any other gathering of citizens whatever it may be. By the exercise of this ability you will have the doctor and the trainer as your slaves, and your man of business will turn out to be making money not for himself but for another; for you, in fact, who have the ability to speak and to convince the masses.

453 SOCRATES. Now, Gorgias, I think that you have defined with great precision what you take the art of oratory to be, and, if I understand you aright, you are saying that oratory is productive of conviction, and that this is the be-all and end-all of its whole activity. Or have you some further power to ascribe to oratory beyond that of producing conviction in the souls of its hearers?

GORGIAS. No, Socrates; the definition which you have given seems to be quite adequate; that is the main point about oratory.

SOCRATES. Listen now, Gorgias. If ever any man made it his object in conversation to know exactly what the conversation is about, I am quite sure – and you may be sure too – that I am such a man, and I believe that I should be right in saying that you are another.

GORGIAS. What follows from that, Socrates?

SOCRATES. I'll tell you. This conviction produced by oratory that you speak of – I really have no clear knowledge what it is or what it is conviction about. I won't say that I haven't a suspicion of your meaning on both points, but that suspicion won't prevent me from asking you what you believe to be the nature of the conviction produced by oratory and the subject of that conviction. You may wonder why, if I have this suspicion, I ask you instead of answering the question myself. I am moved to do so not by any consideration personal to you but by consideration for the argument, which I wish to proceed in such a way as to place before us in the clearest possible light what we are talking about. I think that you will agree that my questions are fair if you look at the matter like this. Suppose I were asking you what sort of painter Zeuxis[1] is, and you replied that he is a painter of pictures; wouldn't it be quite reasonable for me to ask what sort of pictures he paints?

GORGIAS. Certainly.

SOCRATES. Because there are other painters who paint many other kinds of picture?

GORGIAS. Yes.

SOCRATES. But if Zeuxis were the only picture painter your answer would have been right?

GORGIAS. Of course.

---

1. Zeuxis was famous in particular for his accurate rendering of natural objects. He is compared by Aristotle unfavourably with Polygnotus as a creator of ideal form rather than of ideal character.

SOCRATES. Well, now take oratory. Do you think that oratory is the only art that creates conviction or do other arts create it as well? For example, does a man who teaches any subject create conviction or not?

GORGIAS. Of course he does, Socrates; unquestionably.

SOCRATES. Again, if we take the other arts mentioned just now, do not arithmetic and the arithmetician teach us all that concerns number?

GORGIAS. Certainly.

SOCRATES. And therefore also create conviction?

GORGIAS. Yes.

SOCRATES. Then arithmetic as well as oratory produces conviction?

GORGIAS. It would seem so.

SOCRATES. And if we are asked what sort of conviction and conviction about what, we shall say conviction of the kind created by teaching about odd and even and their magnitude. And similarly with all the other arts we mentioned; we shall be able to show, shan't we, not only that they produce conviction but also the nature and subject of that conviction?

GORGIAS. Yes.

SOCRATES. Then oratory is not the only creator of conviction.

GORGIAS. True.

SOCRATES. Then, since other arts besides oratory discharge this function, we shall be right to ask next, as we did about the painter, the nature and subject of the conviction which is the peculiar province of oratory. Don't you agree?

GORGIAS. Yes.

SOCRATES. Answer then, Gorgias, since you share my opinion.

GORGIAS. Oratory serves, Socrates, to produce the kind of conviction needed in courts of law and other

454

large assemblies, and the subject of this kind of conviction is right and wrong.

SOCRATES. That is just what I suspected you meant, Gorgias. But don't be surprised if later on I repeat this procedure and ask additional questions when the answer seems to be already clear. My motive, as I say, is not in the least personal; it is simply to help the discussion to progress towards its end in a logical sequence and to prevent us from getting into the habit of anticipating one another's statements because we have a vague suspicion what they are likely to be, instead of allowing you to develop your argument in your own way from the agreed premises.

GORGIAS. A thoroughly sound method, Socrates.

SOCRATES. Now take this point. You would agree that there is such a thing as 'knowing'?

GORGIAS. Certainly.

SOCRATES. And such a thing as 'believing'?

GORGIAS. Yes.

SOCRATES. Well, do you think that knowing and believing are the same, or is there a difference between knowledge and belief?

GORGIAS. I should say that there is a difference.

SOCRATES. Quite right; and you can prove it like this. If you were asked whether there are such things as true and false beliefs, you would say that there are, no doubt.

GORGIAS. Yes.

SOCRATES. But are there such things as true and false knowledge?

GORGIAS. Certainly not.

SOCRATES. Then knowledge and belief are clearly not the same thing.

GORGIAS. True.

SOCRATES. Yet men who believe may just as properly be called convinced as men who know?

GORGIAS. Yes.

SOCRATES. May we then posit the existence of two kinds of conviction, one which gives knowledge and one which gives belief without knowledge?

GORGIAS. Certainly.

SOCRATES. Now which kind of conviction about right and wrong is created by oratory in courts of law and elsewhere, the kind which engenders knowledge or the kind which engenders belief without knowledge?

GORGIAS. The kind which engenders belief, obviously.

SOCRATES. So it appears that the conviction which oratory produces about right and wrong is of the kind which is followed by belief, not the kind which arises from teaching?

GORGIAS. Yes.

SOCRATES. And the orator does not teach juries and other bodies about right and wrong – he merely persuades them; he could hardly teach so large a number of people matters of such importance in a short time.

GORGIAS. Of course he couldn't.

SOCRATES. Come now, let us see what our statements about oratory really amount to; I don't mind admitting that for my own part I still haven't a clear idea what I think about it. When the citizens hold a meeting to appoint medical officers or shipbuilders or any other professional class of person,[1] surely it won't be the orator who advises them then. Obviously in every such election the choice ought to fall on the most expert; if it is a question of building walls or establishing harbours or dockyards, it is architects whose opinion will be asked;

---

1. It was customary in some Greek cities to appoint a noted doctor as a public servant, paid from public funds and receiving no fees from individual patients. Such an appointment would be the object of keen competition; see below, p. 127. Shipbuilders and the like presumably competed for public contracts on particular occasions.

if it is the appointment of generals or the order of battle against an enemy or the capture of strongholds that is being debated, men of experience in war will be called on for advice, not orators. What is your opinion about this, Gorgias? You claim to be an orator and capable of producing orators; so I naturally look to you for information about your own art. And in doing so I have your interests at heart as well, believe me. It may be that there is someone present now who wishes to be your pupil; in fact I see that there are several such, but they are perhaps shy of putting questions to you. Imagine then that they as well as I are saying to you: 'What advantage shall we gain, Gorgias, if we take lessons from you? What shall we be able to advise our fellow-citizens about? Simply about right and wrong, or about the other subjects too which Socrates has mentioned?' Try to give them an answer.

GORGIAS. I will try, Socrates, to reveal to you clearly the whole power of oratory; your own remarks make an admirable introduction. You know of course that Athens owes its dockyards and walls and harbour establishments partly to the advice of Themistocles and partly to that of Pericles, not in any degree to that of the professional builders.

SOCRATES. That is what we are told about Themistocles, Gorgias. As for Pericles, I heard him myself when he was proposing the building of the middle wall.[1]

GORGIAS. And you can see that when there is a choice   456 to be made of the kind that you spoke of just now it is the orators who dictate policy and get their proposals adopted.

1. In 479 B.C., after the Persian Wars, the Athenians refortified Athens and the port of Piraeus at the instance of Themistocles. Later, in 458, to guard against Athens being cut off from the sea in the event of war, two diverging long walls were built

SOCRATES. I do see it, and it fills me with amazement, Gorgias. That is why I have been asking you all this time what the power of oratory consists in. To judge by what it effects it seems practically supernatural.

GORGIAS. You might well be amazed, Socrates, if you knew the whole truth and realized that oratory embraces and controls almost all other spheres of human activity. I can give you a striking illustration of this. It has often happened that I have gone with my brother and other doctors to visit some sick person who refused to drink his medicine or to submit to surgery or cautery, and when the doctors could not persuade him I have succeeded, simply by my use of the art of oratory. I tell you that, if in any city that you like to name, an orator and a doctor had to compete before the Assembly or any other body for the appointment of medical officer, the man who could speak would be appointed by an overwhelming vote if he wanted the post, and the doctor would be nowhere. Similarly if he had to compete with any other professional man the orator could get himself appointed against any opposition; there is no subject on which he could not speak before a popular audience more persuasively than any professional of whatever kind.

Such is the nature and power of the art of oratory, Socrates, but there are of course limits to its proper use, as there are to the use of any other accomplishment. Just because a man has acquired such skill in boxing or all-in wrestling or armed combat that he can beat anyone, friend or foe, is no reason why he

---

from the city to the coast, the northern running to Piraeus and the southern to Phalerum. Finally, on the advice of Pericles, the southern wall was abandoned, and the so-called 'middle' wall was built parallel and close to the northern wall, and like it joining the fortifications of Piraeus. The effect was to make Athens and Piraeus a single fortress.

should employ it against all men indiscriminately
and strike and wound and kill his friends. And, on
the other hand, if a course of physical training has
put a man in good condition and made him a boxer,
and he then strikes his father or mother or some
relation or friend, that is no reason for detesting
and banishing trainers and those who teach the use
of weapons. They gave instruction intending that
it should be put to a good use against the country's
enemies and against wrong-doers, defensively, not
aggressively, and if their pupils on the contrary make   457
a bad use of their strength and skill it does not follow
that the teachers are criminal or the art which they
teach culpable and wicked; the fault rests with those
who do not make a proper use of it. The same
argument holds good about oratory. The orator
can speak on any subject against any opposition in
such a way as to prevail on any topic he chooses,
but the fact that he possesses the power to deprive
doctors and other professional men of their reputation does not justify him in doing so; he is as much
bound to make a proper use of his oratory as the
possessor of physical superiority. But if a man who
has acquired oratorical skill uses the power which
his art confers to do wrong, that is no reason to
detest and banish his teacher. His instruction was
given to be employed for good ends, and if the
pupil uses it for the opposite it is he, not the man
who taught him, who deserves detestation and
banishment and death.

SOCRATES. I suppose, Gorgias, that like me you must
have been present at many arguments, and have
observed how difficult the parties find it to define
exactly the subject which they have taken in hand
and to come away from their discussion mutually
enlightened; what usually happens is that, as soon
as they disagree and one declares the other to be

mistaken or obscure in what he says, they lose their temper and accuse one another of speaking from motives of personal spite and in an endeavour to score a victory rather than to investigate the question at issue; and sometimes they part on the worst possible terms, after such an exchange of abuse that the bystanders feel vexed on their own account that they ever thought it worth their while to listen to such people. You may wonder why I am saying this. It is because what you are saying now does not appear to me quite consistent with what you said at first about oratory, and I am afraid that if I probe the matter further you may suppose that my purpose is not so much to elucidate the subject as to win a verbal victory over you. If you are the same sort of person as myself, I will willingly go on questioning you; otherwise I will stop. If you ask what I mean, I am one of those people who are glad to have their own mistakes pointed out and glad to point out the mistakes of others, but who would just as soon have the first experience as the second; in fact I consider the first a greater gain, inasmuch as it is better to be relieved of very bad trouble oneself than to relieve another, and in my opinion no worse trouble can befall a man than to have a false belief about the subjects which we are now discussing. So if you are of the same mind, let us go on with the conversation; but if you think that we ought to abandon it let us drop it at once and bring the argument to an end.

GORGIAS. Personally, Socrates, I would claim to be just the sort of person you have indicated, but perhaps we ought to consider the rest of the company. Before your arrival I had already given them a long demonstration, and it may perhaps take us too far to go on with this argument. We ought to consult their wishes as well as our own; it may be that we are keeping some of them when they have other things to do.

CHAEREPHON. You can judge for yourselves by the noise they are making, Gorgias and Socrates, that everybody is anxious to hear whatever you may have to say. For my part, God forbid that I should ever be so busy as to have to abandon for something more important a discussion so interesting as this and so ably conducted.

CALLICLES. I agree most emphatically, Chaerephon. I too have been present at many discussions, but I don't believe that any has ever given me so much pleasure as this. If you like to go on talking all day, I shall be only too pleased.

SOCRATES. Well, there is no obstacle on my side, Callicles, if Gorgias is willing.

GORGIAS. It would be a disgrace for me not to be willing, Socrates, after my spontaneous offer to reply to any question. So, if our friends approve, go on with the conversation and ask me anything you like.

SOCRATES. Let me explain the point which surprised me in what you said, Gorgias; it may be that you were right and I didn't understand you properly. You say that you can make an orator of anyone who likes to learn from you?

GORGIAS. Yes.

SOCRATES. And consequently he will be able to get his way before a popular audience not by instructing but by convincing?

GORGIAS. Certainly.

459

SOCRATES. You said just now that even on matters of health the orator will be more convincing than the doctor.

GORGIAS. Before a popular audience – yes, I did.

SOCRATES. A popular audience means an ignorant audience, doesn't it? He won't be more convincing than the doctor before experts, I presume.

GORGIAS. True.

SOCRATES. Now, if he is more convincing than the doctor he is more convincing than the expert?

GORGIAS. Naturally.

SOCRATES. Not being a doctor, of course?

GORGIAS. Of course not.

SOCRATES. And the non-doctor, presumably, is ignorant of what the doctor knows?

GORGIAS. Obviously.

SOCRATES. So when the orator is more convincing than the doctor, what happens is that an ignorant person is more convincing than the expert before an equally ignorant audience. Am I right?

GORGIAS. That is what happens in that case, no doubt.

SOCRATES. And the same will be true of the orator in relation to all the other arts. The orator need have no knowledge of the truth about things; it is enough for him to have discovered a knack of convincing the ignorant that he knows more than the experts.

GORGIAS. And isn't it a great comfort, Socrates, to be able to meet specialists in all the other arts on equal terms without going to the trouble of acquiring more than this single one?

SOCRATES. We will discuss in a moment, if it turns out to be relevant, whether this does in fact put the orator on equal terms with the others or not; but first of all let us consider how he stands with regard to right and wrong, honour and dishonour, good and bad. Is he in the same position here as he is about medicine and the objects of the other arts, quite ignorant of the actual nature of good and bad or honour and dishonour or right and wrong, but possessed of a power of persuasion which enables him, in spite of his ignorance, to appear to the ignorant wiser than those who know? Or must he have knowledge and understanding of all these matters before he comes to you to be taught oratory?

It is not your business, as a professor of oratory, to teach your pupil about these things. Will you then, if he comes to you ignorant of them, enable him to acquire a popular reputation for knowledge and goodness when in fact he possesses neither, or will you be quite unable to teach him oratory at all unless he knows the truth about these things beforehand? What are we to think about all this, Gorgias? Do, in heaven's name, perform the promise you made a short time ago and disclose to us what the power of oratory is. 460

GORGIAS. I suppose, Socrates, that I shall have to teach a pupil those things as well, if he happens not to know them.

SOCRATES. Stop there; that is an excellent answer. If you are to make a man an orator, he must either know right and wrong before he comes to you or learn them from you after becoming your pupil.

GORGIAS. Certainly.

SOCRATES. Well now, a man who has learnt carpentry is a carpenter, isn't he?

GORGIAS. Yes.

SOCRATES. And a man who has learnt music a musician?

GORGIAS. Yes.

SOCRATES. And a man who has learnt medicine a doctor, and so on. In fact, a man who has learnt any subject possesses the character which knowledge of that subject confers.

GORGIAS. Of course.

SOCRATES. Then by the same reckoning a man who has learnt about right will be righteous?[1]

GORGIAS. Unquestionably.

1. This argument depends on the assumption regularly made by Socrates and only slightly modified by Plato that all wrongdoing is the result of ignorance, and that perfect knowledge of what is right must inevitably issue in perfect conduct.

SOCRATES. And a righteous man performs right actions, I presume.

GORGIAS. Yes.

SOCRATES. He will in fact of necessity always will to perform right actions.

GORGIAS. Apparently.

SOCRATES. Then the righteous man will never will to do wrong.

GORGIAS. Never.

SOCRATES. And according to the argument the orator must be righteous.

GORGIAS. Yes.

SOCRATES. Then the orator will never will to do wrong.

GORGIAS. Apparently not.

SOCRATES. Now do you remember that you said a short time ago that if a boxer makes a bad use of his skill that is no reason for blaming his trainers and sending them into exile, and similarly if an orator employs his oratory for a bad end we ought not to blame or banish his teacher, but the man who actually does wrong and uses his art amiss. You did say that, didn't you?

GORGIAS. I did.

SOCRATES. But now it appears, doesn't it, that this same orator would never have done wrong in any circumstances?

GORGIAS. Yes.

SOCRATES. Moreover, at the beginning of our discussion, Gorgias, it was stated that oratory was concerned with speech, not speech about odd and even but speech about right and wrong. Do you remember?

GORGIAS. Yes.

SOCRATES. When you were saying that, I got the notion that oratory could never be a bad thing because it is always talking about right. But when shortly afterwards you said that an orator might make a wrong use of oratory I was surprised at the inconsistency, and it was then, if you recall, that I remarked that if you were like me in counting it a gain to have your mistakes pointed out it would be worth while going on with the conversation, but if not we had better let it drop. You see for yourself that further consideration has led to our agreeing that it is impossible for the orator to make a wrong use of his oratory and to will to do wrong. What are we to make of this? I swear, Gorgias, that it will need more than a short discussion if we are to get properly to the bottom of it.

POLUS. Come, Socrates, can even you really believe what you are saying about oratory? All because Gorgias did not like not to agree with you that the orator must know what is right and honourable and good, and asserted that if a pupil came to him ignorant of these things he would teach him himself. And then this admission on his part made the argument appear inconsistent – just the sort of thing you love, and it was you who gave the discussion this interrogative form. After all, who do you suppose is going to admit that he doesn't know and can't teach the nature of right? It is exceedingly ill-bred to have caused the conversation to take such a turn.

SOCRATES. Polus, my very good friend, it is at just such moments as this that we need the services of friends and sons, so that when we older folk trip up in word or deed you of the younger generation may be there to set us on our feet again. If Gorgias and I have gone astray in our argument, come and set us right – that is just what you are for. And if you think that we are mistaken in any of our conclusions, I'm perfectly willing to take back anything you like, but on one condition.

POLUS. What is that?

SOCRATES. That you keep in check the tendency to make long speeches which you showed at the beginning of our conversation.

POLUS. What? Am I not to be allowed to say as much as I choose?

SOCRATES. It would certainly be hard luck, my good sir, if on arriving in Athens, which allows freedom of speech above all other cities in Greece, you found that you alone were denied that privilege. But, on the other hand, think what hard luck it will be for me if, when you are making a long speech and refusing to answer the question put to you, I am not to be allowed to go away and get out of hearing. If you take any interest in the present argument and want to set it on the right lines, accept my offer to take back any step in it you like, and by asking and answering questions in turn, like Gorgias and myself, examine and be examined alternately. You would claim, I suppose, that you know as much as Gorgias?

POLUS. Yes.

SOCRATES. In that case do you, like Gorgias, invite people to put any question to you, relying on your ability to answer?

POLUS. Certainly.

SOCRATES. Well, would you rather ask or answer at the present moment? Make your choice.

POLUS. I will; *you* shall answer, Socrates. Since you think Gorgias confused about the nature of oratory, tell me what you take oratory to be.

SOCRATES. Are you asking me what sort of art I take it to be?

POLUS. Yes, I am.

SOCRATES. No art at all, Polus, if I'm to give you a perfectly truthful answer.

POLUS. What do you think it is then?

SOCRATES. A thing which you say in a treatise I read lately is the creator of art.[1]

POLUS. What do you mean?

SOCRATES. I should call it a sort of knack gained by experience.

POLUS. You think oratory is a sort of knack?

SOCRATES. Subject to your correction, I do.

POLUS. A knack of doing what?

SOCRATES. Producing a kind of gratification and pleasure.

POLUS. In that case, if it is able to give men gratification, don't you consider it a fine thing?

SOCRATES. My dear Polus, do you feel so adequately informed already of my views on the nature of oratory that you pass on to the subsidiary question whether I consider it a fine thing?

POLUS. Didn't you tell me that you consider it a sort of knack?

SOCRATES. You set a high value on giving gratification; will you gratify me in a small matter?

POLUS. By all means.

SOCRATES. Just ask me, will you, what sort of art I take cookery to be.

POLUS. Very well; what sort of art is cookery?

SOCRATES. It isn't an art at all, Polus.

POLUS. What is it then? Explain.

SOCRATES. A kind of knack gained by experience, I should say.

POLUS. A knack of doing what, pray?

SOCRATES. Producing gratification and pleasure, Polus.

POLUS. Then are oratory and cookery the same thing?

SOCRATES. Certainly not, but they are branches of the same occupation.

POLUS. What occupation do you mean?

SOCRATES. I'm afraid that the truth may sound rather

1. Cf. p. 21 above.

uncivil, and I wouldn't like Gorgias to think that I am making fun of his profession. It may be that this isn't the sort of oratory that he practises; our argument just now shed no light on his own views on the subject. But what I call oratory is a branch of something which certainly isn't a fine or honourable pursuit.

GORGIAS. What do you mean, Socrates? Speak out and don't be afraid of hurting my feelings.

SOCRATES. Well, Gorgias, the whole of which oratory is a branch seems to me to be a pursuit which has nothing to do with art, but which requires in its practitioners a shrewd and bold spirit together with a natural aptitude for dealing with men. The generic name which I should give it is pandering; it has many subdivisions, one of which is cookery, an occupation which masquerades as an art but in my opinion is no more than a knack acquired by routine. I should classify oratory and beauty-culture and popular lecturing as species of the same genus; there you have four distinct branches with four distinct fields of activity. If Polus likes to question me about this he is welcome to do so; it doesn't seem to have struck him that I have not yet explained where I place oratory among the subdivisions of pandering. He goes on to ask the further question whether I don't think oratory an honourable pursuit, but it would be quite improper for me to say whether I think oratory honourable or the reverse before I have explained what it really is. However, if you care to ask me, Polus, where oratory stands among the subdivisions of pandering, ask away.

POLUS. Very well then; what branch of pandering is oratory?

SOCRATES. I'm not sure that you will understand the answer. In my view oratory is a spurious counterfeit of a branch of the art of government.

POLUS. And would you call it honourable or dishonourable?

SOCRATES. Dishonourable undoubtedly, if you insist on an answer, for I would call anything that is bad dishonourable. But this is to assume that you have already grasped my meaning.

GORGIAS. If it comes to that, Socrates, I don't understand your meaning any better than Polus.

SOCRATES. Of course you don't, Gorgias; I haven't yet made it plain. But our friend Polus has all the impatience of youth.

GORGIAS. Never mind him; tell *me* what you mean when you call oratory a spurious counterfeit of a branch of the art of government.

SOCRATES, Well, I'll try to explain my view of the nature of oratory; if I'm wrong Polus will correct me. We may assume, I suppose, the existence of body and soul?

464

GORGIAS. Of course.

SOCRATES. And you would agree that there is bodily health and spiritual health?

GORGIAS. Yes.

SOCRATES. And also such a thing as an unreal appearance of health? For example, many people appear to enjoy health in whom nobody but a doctor or trainer could detect the reverse.

GORGIAS. True.

SOCRATES. I maintain that there is a condition of soul as well as body which gives the appearance of health without the reality.

GORGIAS. Quite right.

SOCRATES. Now I'll put my meaning in a clearer light, if I can. I maintain that these two, body and soul, have two arts corresponding to them; that which deals with the soul I call the art of government, but though the subject of physical welfare constitutes a unity I cannot find a single name for the art which deals with the body, and which has two branches, training and medicine. In the art of government what corresponds to training is called legislation and what corresponds to medicine the administration of justice. The members of each of these pairs, training and medicine, legislation and justice, have something in common, because they are concerned with the same object, but they are different from one another none the less. We have then these four arts, constantly concerned with the highest welfare of body and soul respectively; and the pseudo-art of the pander, being instinctively aware of this division of function though it has no accurate knowledge, divides itself also into four branches, and putting on the guise of each of the genuine arts pretends to be the art which it is impersonating. The difference is that pandering pays no regard to the welfare of its object, but catches fools with the bait of ephemeral pleasure and tricks them into holding it in the highest esteem. Thus, cookery puts on the mask of medicine and pretends to know what foods are best for the body, and, if an audience of children or of men with no more sense than children had to decide whether a confectioner or a doctor is the better judge of wholesome and unwholesome foodstuffs, the doctor would unquestionably die of hunger. Now I call this sort of thing pandering and I declare that it is dishonourable – I'm speaking to you now, Polus – because it makes pleasure its aim instead of good, and I maintain that it is merely a knack and not an art because it has no rational account to give of the nature of the various things which it offers. I refuse to give the title of art to anything irrational, and if you want to raise an objection on this point I am ready to justify my position.

465

Cookery then, as I say, is the form of pandering which corresponds to medicine, and in the same way physical training has its counterfeit in beauty-culture, a mischievous, swindling, base, servile trade, which creates an illusion by the use of artificial adjuncts and make-up and depilatories and costume, and makes people assume a borrowed beauty to the neglect of the true beauty which is the product of training. In short, I will put the matter in the form of a geometrical proportion – perhaps now you will be able to follow me – and say that cookery is to medicine as beauty-culture is to physical training, or rather that popular lecturing is to legislation as beauty-culture to training, and oratory to justice as cookery to medicine. There is, I repeat, an essential difference between lecturing and oratory, but because they border on one another their practitioners are liable to be confused in the popular mind as occupying common ground and being engaged in the same pursuit; in fact lecturers and orators no more know what to make of one another than the world at large knows what to make of them. The same confusion would occur with cookery and medicine if the body were left to its own devices instead of being controlled by the soul, which distinguishes the two from its superior viewpoint; if the body had to draw this distinction with no criterion but its own sensations of pleasure, the saying of Anaxagoras – with which you are so well acquainted, Polus – would have more than one application. 'All things would be indistinguishably mixed together', and there would be no boundaries between the provinces of medicine and cookery.[1]

Now you know my view of the nature of oratory;

1. Anaxagoras deduced the variety of the existing world from a primary mixture, and the words 'All things were together' apparently formed the opening of his treatise. The point of the reference here is that in Anaxagoras' system the first impulse to the differentiation of the mixtures was given by mind.

it is to the soul what cookery is to the body. Perhaps it may seem strange that after forbidding you to make a long speech I should have spun out my own to such a length. My excuse is that when I spoke more briefly you didn't understand; you couldn't make anything of the answer I gave you and begged for an explanation. If I in my turn find myself in difficulties about your answers, you too shall develop them more fully; otherwise it is only reasonable to let me be content with them as they are. And now if you have any point to make about what I have said, fire away.

466

POLUS. Very well; you say that oratory is pandering?

SOCRATES. I said that it was a branch of pandering. Your memory is very bad for someone so young, Polus. What will happen to you by and by?

POLUS. And do you think that good orators are meanly thought of in a state, and regarded as panders?[1]

SOCRATES. Is this a question or the beginning of a speech?

POLUS. A question.

SOCRATES. In my opinion they are not thought of at all.

POLUS. Not thought of? Have they not very great power in a state?

SOCRATES. If by power you mean something that is a benefit to its possessor, no.

POLUS. That is what I do mean.

SOCRATES. Then in that case I consider orators the least powerful people in a state.

POLUS. But can they not kill whoever they please,

1. Polus, instead of grappling with the theory of the nature of oratory put forward by Socrates, characteristically appeals to the esteem in which orators are popularly held. A transition is thus effected to a discussion of the real meaning of power, which leads in turn to the main thesis of the dialogue that 'it is better to suffer wrong than to do wrong'.

like dictators, and inflict confiscation and banishment on anyone they choose?

SOCRATES. I swear, Polus, whenever you open your
mouth I'm in doubt whether you are expressing
your own opinion or asking me a question.

POLUS. I'm asking you a question.

SOCRATES. In that case you are asking me two questions at once, my friend.

POLUS. Two questions? What do you mean?

SOCRATES. Didn't you say just now that orators,
like dictators, can kill whoever they please and
inflict confiscation and banishment on anyone they
choose?

POLUS. Yes.

SOCRATES. Well, I maintain that there are two questions here, and I will answer them both. In my view,
Polus, as I have already said, orators and dictators
are the least powerful persons in a state. They do
practically nothing that they will, only what they
think best.

POLUS. Well, isn't that to enjoy great power?

SOCRATES. According to Polus, no.

POLUS. According to me? But I say it is.

SOCRATES. Oh dear no, you don't. You said that
great power was a benefit to its possessor.

POLUS. So it is.

SOCRATES. Well, do you think it a benefit when a
man devoid of wisdom does what seems best to
him? Do you call that great power?

POLUS. No.

SOCRATES. Then you must prove me wrong, and
show that orators are men of wisdom, and oratory   467
an art and not mere pandering. Otherwise orators
who do what they please in a state, and dictators
too, for that matter, will have nothing to congratu-
late themselves upon, since according to you power
is a blessing, but doing what one pleases without

49

wisdom is by your own admission a curse. You did admit that, didn't you?

POLUS. Yes.

SOCRATES. Then unless Polus can show Socrates that he was wrong and prove that orators and dictators do what they really will, how can they be said to enjoy great power in a state?

POLUS. This fellow –

SOCRATES. Says that they don't do what they really will. Prove me wrong.

POLUS. Didn't you admit just now that they do what seems best to them?

SOCRATES. Certainly; I don't retract it.

POLUS. Then don't they do what they will?

SOCRATES. No.

POLUS. Although they do what they please?

SOCRATES. Yes.

POLUS. What you say is monstrous and outrageous, Socrates.

SOCRATES. Don't use hard words, my peerless Polus, if I may address you for once in your own alliterative style. Prove my mistake by your questions, if you still have any to ask, or else let us change parts, and you do the answering.

POLUS. Very well, I don't mind answering, in order to get at your meaning.

SOCRATES. Do you think that when men act they will their act itself or the object of their act? Take, for example, patients who drink medicine by doctor's orders. Do you think that they will the act of drinking the medicine with its attendant disagreeableness or the object of the act, that is, health?

POLUS. Health, obviously.

SOCRATES. Similarly, men who trade abroad or engage in business do not will what they are doing at the time; who would will the risk of a voyage and the troubles of business? What they will, I imagine, is the object of their voyage, to make a fortune; it is wealth that they sail abroad for.

POLUS. Certainly.

SOCRATES. And is not the same universally true? When a man performs an act as a means to an end, he wills not his act, but the object of his act.

POLUS. Yes.

SOCRATES. Now is there anything which is not either good or bad or intermediate and neutral?

POLUS. Everything must necessarily fall into one or other of these categories, Socrates.

SOCRATES. Would you call wisdom and health and riches and the like good, and their opposites bad?

POLUS. Certainly.

SOCRATES. And would you place in the intermediate class such things as the following, which partake sometimes of the nature of good, sometimes of bad, and sometimes of neither; I mean, for example, 468 sitting and walking and running and sailing, or, to take things of a different type, wood and stone and the like? Are these what you mean when you say that some things are neither good nor bad?

POLUS. Precisely.

SOCRATES. Now do men perform these neutral acts as a means to the good, or *vice versa*?

POLUS. The former, obviously.

SOCRATES. Then when we walk we walk as a means to the good, because we think it the better course; and when we stand still on the other hand we stand still from the same motive as a means to the good. Do you agree?

POLUS. Yes.

SOCRATES. And when we kill or banish or confiscate, if we ever do so, we act from a belief that it is better for us to do so than not?

POLUS. Certainly.

SOCRATES. Then men do all these things as a means to the good?

POLUS. Yes.

SOCRATES. We agreed, didn't we, that we do not will acts that are means, but the ends to which they are means?

POLUS. Of course.

SOCRATES. So we do not will a man's death or banishment or loss of property simply for its own sake; we will it if it brings advantage, but not if it brings the reverse. As you say yourself, we will what is good; we do not will what is indifferent, still less what is bad. Am I right, Polus, or not? Why don't you answer?

POLUS. You are right.

SOCRATES. Then, if that is granted, when a dictator or an orator kills or banishes or confiscates because he believes it to be to his advantage, and it turns out to be to his disadvantage, we must allow that he does what he pleases, mustn't we?

POLUS. Yes.

SOCRATES. But does he do what he wills, when what he does turns out to be bad? Why don't you answer?

POLUS. I agree that he doesn't do what he wills.

SOCRATES. How can one say then that such a man has great power in the state, when by your own admission great power is an advantage to its possessor?

POLUS. One can't.

SOCRATES. So it appears that I was right when I said that a man may do what he pleases in a state without either having great power or doing what he wills?

POLUS. To listen to you, Socrates, one might think that you wouldn't be glad to have the opportunity of doing what you please in the state rather than not, and that you don't envy a man who can kill or confiscate or imprison at will.

SOCRATES. Justly or unjustly, do you mean?

POLUS. It makes no difference; he's enviable in either
case, isn't he?

SOCRATES. Take care what you are saying, Polus.

POLUS. Why?

SOCRATES. Because it's wrong to speak like this of men who are unenviable and miserable; they are rather to be pitied.

POLUS. Do you really believe that about the people I am speaking of?

SOCRATES. Of course.

POLUS. You think that a man who kills whom he pleases, and is right to do so, is miserable and pitiable?

SOCRATES. No, but I don't call him enviable.

POLUS. A moment ago you called him miserable, didn't you?

SOCRATES. I meant the man who kills wrongfully, my friend. Him I call pitiable as well as miserable. But I don't envy the man who kills with right on his side.

POLUS. A man who is put to death wrongfully is pitiable and miserable, I suppose.

SOCRATES. Less so than the man who kills him, Polus, or the man who is put to death because he deserves it.

POLUS. How so, Socrates?

SOCRATES. Because the greatest of all misfortunes is to do wrong.

POLUS. But surely it is worse to suffer wrong?

SOCRATES. Certainly not.

POLUS. Do you mean to say that you would rather suffer wrong than do wrong?

SOCRATES. I would rather avoid both; but if I had to choose one or the other I would rather suffer wrong than do wrong.

POLUS. Then you wouldn't like to be a dictator?

SOCRATES. I certainly wouldn't if your notion of a dictator is the same as mine.

POLUS. I mean by a dictator, I repeat, a man who can do whatever he pleases in the state, killing and banishing and having his own way in everything.

SOCRATES. My good friend, hear what I have to say and raise objections if you like. Suppose I were to meet you in the market-place in the middle of the morning with a dagger up my sleeve, and say: 'Polus, I've just acquired a simply wonderful instrument of dictatorship. Such is my power that if I decide that any of the people you see around you should die on the spot, die he shall; or if I think that any of them ought to have his head broken or his clothes torn, it's as good as done.' If on top of that, to convince you, I were to display my dagger, you would probably reply: 'At that rate, Socrates, anybody can exercise great power; houses can be burnt down at will, and the dockyards and triremes of the Athenian navy and all the merchant ships in public and private ownership.' So it appears that doing what one pleases is not the same as having great power, is it?

POLUS. Not in this case, certainly.

470 SOCRATES. Can you tell me what the flaw is in this kind of power?

POLUS. Yes.

SOCRATES. What is it then?

POLUS. It is that a man who behaves like this is bound to be punished.

SOCRATES. And being punished is a misfortune?

POLUS. Of course.

SOCRATES. Then, my good sir, you come back again to the conclusion that doing what one pleases can only be called a blessing and really deserve the name of power if the action is attended by advantage to the actor; otherwise it is a bad and feeble thing. Look at the matter in this light. We agreed, didn't we, that the actions which we mentioned just now killing and banishing and confiscating, are sometimes to a man's advantage and sometimes not?

POLUS. Certainly.

SOCRATES. Then here, it seems, we have one point on which we are agreed?

POLUS. Yes.

SOCRATES. Can you tell when these actions will bring advantage? How do you draw the line?

POLUS. I would rather you answered this question yourself, Socrates.

SOCRATES. Just as you please. I should say that when these actions are right they bring advantage, and when they are wrong, the reverse.

POLUS. You're a hard man to get the better of, Socrates, but even a child could prove that you are mistaken here.

SOCRATES. Then I shall be very grateful to the child, and equally so to you, if you will show me my mistake and cure me of my silliness. Don't be backward in doing a kindness to a friend. Prove me wrong.

POLUS. I can do that, Socrates, without resorting to ancient history. The events of the quite recent past are enough to refute you and to show that many wrong-doers are happy.

SOCRATES. What events do you mean?

POLUS. Well, look at Archelaus the son of Perdiccas ruling in Macedonia.[1]

SOCRATES. I've heard of him anyhow even if I can't look at him.

POLUS. Do you think that he is happy or miserable?

1. Archelaus, the illegitimate son of Perdiccas II, succeeded his father c. 413 B.C. and reigned till 399, when he was assassinated. In spite of his crimes he was in many ways an enlightened ruler, whose ability is praised by Thucydides and who did much to spread Greek influence in Macedonia. He invited famous Greek artists, including Zeuxis, to his court, and Euripides died there.

SOCRATES. I don't know, Polus; I've never met him.

POLUS. Do you mean that you can't tell at once even from this distance, without meeting him, that he is happy?

SOCRATES. Indeed I can't.

POLUS. Then no doubt you'll say even of the Great King[1] that you don't know whether he is happy, Socrates.

SOCRATES. It will be no more than the truth; I don't know what degree of enlightenment and virtue he has attained.

POLUS. What? Does happiness depend entirely on that?

SOCRATES. Yes, Polus, in my opinion it does; I maintain that men and women are happy if they are honourable and upright, but miserable if they are vicious and wicked.

471 POLUS. Then by your account, Archelaus is miserable.

SOCRATES. If he is vicious, my friend, certainly.

POLUS. Of course he is vicious. He had no claim to the throne he now possesses; his mother was a slave of Alcetas the brother of Perdiccas, and by rights he too was Alcetas' slave; if he had chosen to follow the path of virtue he would be Alcetas' slave still and, according to you, happy. But as things are he is inconceivably miserable, because he has committed enormous crimes. First of all, he sent for this same Alcetas, who was his uncle as well as his master, on the pretence that he would surrender to him the throne of which Perdiccas had deprived him. When he had entertained him and made him drunk, together with his son Alexander, who was his cousin and almost the same age as himself, he flung them both into a cart and took them out by night and murdered them, so that they were never

1. The King of Persia was commonly called the Great King.

heard of again. So far was he from repenting of these crimes and realizing that he had become utterly miserable that shortly afterwards he refused another chance to make himself happy. He had a brother, Perdiccas' legitimate son, a child about seven years old, whom duty required that he should bring up and place on the throne. Instead he threw him into a well and drowned him, and told his mother Cleopatra that he had fallen into the well and been killed while he was running after a goose. So now, as the greatest criminal in the country, far from being the happiest Macedonian alive, he is the most miserable, and no doubt there are a number of Athenians, beginning with you, who would prefer to be any Macedonian, however obscure, rather than Archelaus.

SOCRATES. I said at the beginning of our conversation, Polus, that while I thought you admirably well-trained in oratory you seemed to me to have neglected the art of reasoning. Is this really the argument by which a child could prove and by which in your opinion *you* have now proved that I was wrong when I said that a bad man is not happy? How can this be, my good sir, seeing that I don't admit the force of anything that you have said?

POLUS. Won't admit, it, you mean; in your heart you think as I do.

SOCRATES. The fact is, my dear sir, that you are trying to prove me wrong by the use of oratory, like people in the law courts. They think there that they have got the better of the other party when they can produce a number of respectable witnesses to what they say, while their opponent can produce only one or none at all. But this kind of proof is useless in establishing the truth; it can easily happen that a man is overborn by the false evidence of several apparently respectable persons. In the present case, 472 for instance, practically the whole population of Athens, both native and alien, will agree with you that I am not speaking the truth, if you like to call them as witnesses; you can get, if you wish, the support of Nicias the son of Niceratus and his brothers, who have a row of tripods standing to their credit in the precinct of Dionysus;[1] you can get Aristocrates the son of Scellius, who dedicated that splendid offering in the sanctuary of Pythian Apollo;[2] you can get the whole family of Pericles or any other famous Athenian clan that you care to choose. For all that I, though I am but a single individual, do not agree with you. You produce no compelling reason why I should; you merely call a number of false witnesses against me in your attempt to deprive me of my lawful property, the truth. I believe that nothing worth speaking of will have been accomplished in our discussion unless I can obtain your adhesion, and yours alone, to the truth of what I say; and the same holds good for you, in my opinion, unless you can get my individual suffrage, without regard to what the rest of the world may say.

There are then these two sorts of proof, the kind in which you and many other people believe, and the kind which I on my side think conclusive. Let

1. Nicias was the highly respected leader of the moderate conservative party at Athens, and perished in 413 B.C. in the disaster of the Sicilian expedition, of which he was the reluctant commander. The tripods would commemorate the discharge by Nicias and his brother of the expensive office of *choragus*, provider of the chorus, at the Athenian dramatic festivals. For the anachronism involved in the mention of Nicias and Aristocrates as still living, cf. Introduction, p. 14.

2. Aristocrates was one of the six commanders executed after the sea battle of Arginusae in 406 for failure to rescue survivors from the water. His offering at Delphi must have been sufficiently magnificent to be well known.

us compare them and note how they differ; the subject of our argument, so far from being trivial, is perhaps that on which knowledge is most honourable and ignorance most disgraceful; it is in brief knowledge or ignorance of who is happy and who is not. First of all, to take the point which is at issue at the moment, you believe that it is possible for a man to be happy who is wicked and acts wickedly, since you believe Archelaus to be wicked but happy. Am I right in taking that to be your position?

POLUS. Absolutely right.

SOCRATES. And I say that it is impossible. Our disagreement turns on this single point. Now what I want to know is this; will a man who does wrong be happy if he is brought to justice and punished?

POLUS. On the contrary, he will then be most miserable.

SOCRATES. But, by your account, if he isn't brought to justice he will be happy?

POLUS. Yes.

SOCRATES. On the other hand, Polus, my opinion is that the wicked man and the doer of wicked acts is miserable in any case, but more miserable if he does not pay the penalty and suffer punishment for his crimes, and less miserable if he does pay the penalty and suffer punishment in this world and the next.

POLUS. What an extraordinary proposition to maintain, Socrates. 473

SOCRATES. I will try nevertheless to make you also concur in this view, my friend, for I have a high regard for you. At the moment the point on which we differ is this – see if you agree. I said earlier that doing wrong is worse than suffering wrong.

POLUS. You did.

SOCRATES. And you that suffering wrong is worse.

POLUS. Yes.

SOCRATES. And I said that wrong-doers are miserable, and you denied it.

POLUS. I certainly did.

SOCRATES. That is your opinion, Polus.

POLUS. And a true opinion too.

SOCRATES. We shall see. You said also that wrong-doers are happy if they escape punishment.

POLUS. Undoubtedly.

SOCRATES. But I said that they are the most miserable of men, and that those who are punished are less miserable. Would you care to refute this proposition?

POLUS. That is an even harder task than you set me before, Socrates.

SOCRATES. Not hard, Polus – impossible; truth can never be refuted.

POLUS. What do you mean? If a man is arrested for the crime of plotting a dictatorship and racked and castrated and blinded with hot irons, and finally, after suffering many other varieties of exquisite torture and seeing his wife and children suffer the same, is crucified or burnt at the stake, will he be happier than if he gets off, establishes himself as dictator, and spends the rest of his life in power doing as he chooses, the object of envy and admiration to natives and foreigners alike? Is this what you maintain that it is impossible to prove untrue?

SOCRATES. You're trying to frighten me with bogeys, my good Polus. You're no more proving me wrong than you were just now, when you appealed to witnesses. Just remind me of a small point; did you say 'arrested for the crime of plotting a dictatorship'?

POLUS. Yes.

SOCRATES. Well, neither the man who establishes a dictatorship by crime nor the man who is punished for attempting to do so can ever be described as the happier; you can't compare the happiness of two people who are both miserable. But the man who gets away with it and becomes a dictator is the more miserable. What's this, Polus? Laughing? Is this a new type of proof, laughing at what your opponent says instead of giving reasons?

POLUS. Do you suppose that reasons are needed, Socrates, when you say things that no one else in the world would say? Ask any of our friends here.

SOCRATES. I'm no politician, Polus. Only last year, when it fell to my lot to be a member of the Council and my tribe was presiding, I had to put a question   474
to the vote, and made myself ridiculous by my ignorance of the correct procedure.[1] Don't ask me to repeat that experience now by taking the votes of the present company, but, if you have no better proof to advance, do as I suggested and put yourself in my hands as I put myself in yours; I will give you a taste of the sort of proof that I believe in.

My method is to call in support of my statements the evidence of a single witness, the man I am arguing with, and to take his vote alone; the rest of the world are nothing to me; I am not talking to them. See now if you are prepared to submit yourself in your turn to examination by answering my questions. I maintain that you and the world in general, as well as I, consider doing wrong worse

1. For the bearing of this episode on the dramatic date of the dialogue, cf. Introduction, p. 13. Any Athenian might be elected by lot a member of the Council, the supreme administrative authority in the state, for one year. The Council numbered five hundred, and the fifty councillors of each of the ten tribes formed a standing committee for the conduct of business during a tenth of the year. During this period a tribe was said to 'preside', and of the councillors of the 'presiding' tribe one was chosen, again by lot, as *epistates* or chairman. Socrates happened to occupy this position on the occasion of the trial of the commanders after Arginusae, when he refused to put an illegal motion to the vote.

than suffering wrong and not being punished worse than being punished.

POLUS. And I say that neither I nor anyone else believes such a thing. Would *you* rather suffer wrong than do wrong?

SOCRATES. Yes, and so would you and so would everybody.

POLUS. On the contrary, neither you nor I nor anybody would make that choice.

SOCRATES. Well, will you answer my questions?

POLUS. Certainly, I am eager to know what you will say.

SOCRATES. If you want to know, answer as if we were beginning again at the beginning. Which do you think the greater evil, Polus, doing wrong or suffering wrong?

POLUS. Suffering wrong.

SOCRATES. And which do you think the baser[1] thing, doing wrong or suffering wrong? Answer.

POLUS. Doing wrong.

SOCRATES. If it is baser, isn't it also the greater evil?

POLUS. Not at all.

SOCRATES. I see. Then you don't consider good identical with fine, or bad with base?

POLUS. No, I don't.

SOCRATES. Here's another question. Have you no standard to which you refer when you apply the word fine to any fine thing, whether it be a body or a colour or a shape or a voice or a mode of behaviour? Take physical beauty first. When you call a body fine are you not referring either to its

---

1. It is necessary for the understanding of the passage which follows to bear in mind that the word *aischron*, here translated 'base' and elsewhere 'dishonourable' or 'shameful', also means 'ugly' and can be used in a physical as well as a moral sense. Similarly *kalon*, which is here opposed to *aischron*, may mean 'beautiful' as well as 'fine' or 'honourable'.

usefulness for some particular purpose or to some feeling of pleasure which makes glad the eyes of its beholders? Is there any reason other than these for calling a body fine?

POLUS. No.

SOCRATES. And similarly with the other things, shapes and colours. You call them fine, don't you, because they are either pleasant or useful or both?

POLUS. Yes.

SOCRATES. And is the same true of voices and musical sounds in general?

POLUS. Yes.

SOCRATES. Now with regard to customs and modes of behaviour; their fineness also presumably depends on their being either useful or pleasant or both.

POLUS. I agree.

SOCRATES. And shall we say the same about the fine- 475 ness of various branches of knowledge?

POLUS. Certainly; your use of pleasure and good as criteria of fineness is excellent, Socrates.[1]

SOCRATES. Then we must define baseness by the opposites of these, that is to say by pain and harm.

POLUS. Unquestionably.

SOCRATES. So when we call one of two fine things the finer, we mean that it surpasses the other either in one or both of these qualities; it is either more pleasant or more useful or both.

POLUS. Certainly.

SOCRATES. And when one of two base things is the baser it must be because it is either more painful or more harmful or both. Do you agree?

POLUS. Yes.

1. Polus believes that the introduction of the criterion of pleasure shows that Socrates is coming round to his opinion. In fact, however, his own use of the term 'good' at this point as a synonym for 'useful' in judging 'fineness' is plainly inconsistent with his refusal above to identify 'base' with 'bad'.

SOCRATES. Now what did we say a moment ago about doing and suffering wrong? You said, I think, that suffering wrong was the greater evil, but doing wrong baser.

POLUS. I did.

SOCRATES. Then if doing wrong is baser than suffering wrong, its greater baseness must inevitably consist in its being either more painful or more harmful or both?

POLUS. There is no escaping that conclusion.

SOCRATES. First, then, let us consider whether doing wrong is more painful than suffering wrong. Do those who do wrong feel more pain than those who suffer wrong?

POLUS. Most certainly not.

SOCRATES. Then doing wrong is not more painful?

POLUS. No.

SOCRATES. And if it is not more painful it cannot be both more painful and more harmful.

POLUS. Of course not.

SOCRATES. Then only the third possibility is left.

POLUS. Yes.

SOCRATES. That is, that it is more harmful.

POLUS. So it seems.

SOCRATES. Then since it involves greater harm doing wrong will be a worse evil than suffering wrong.

POLUS. Obviously.

SOCRATES. Didn't you and I agree before with the universal opinion that doing wrong is a baser thing than suffering wrong?

POLUS. Yes.

SOCRATES. And now it turns out to be a worse evil as well.

POLUS. Apparently.

SOCRATES. Would you then prefer a greater degree of evil and baseness to a lesser? Don't be afraid to answer, Polus. Be a man and submit to the argument as you would to a doctor, and answer 'yes' or 'no' to my question.

POLUS. My answer is 'no' then, Socrates.

SOCRATES. Would anybody prefer it?

POLUS. Not according to this argument.

SOCRATES. I was right then when I said that neither you nor I nor anyone would prefer doing wrong to suffering wrong, since the former turns out to be the greater evil.

POLUS. So it appears.

SOCRATES. You see then, Polus, that when our two methods of proving our points are compared they bear no resemblance to each other. Whereas you have everybody in agreement with you except me, I am content if I can obtain your single agreement and testimony; if I can get your vote I care nothing for those of the rest of the world.

476

So much then for that; now let us consider the second point on which we were at issue, whether being punished for one's misdeeds is the greatest of evils, as you thought, or whether not being punished is a greater, which was my opinion. Look at it like this. Would you say that paying the penalty for one's misdeeds is the same thing as being justly punished?

POLUS. Yes.

SOCRATES. Now can you maintain that what is just is not always fine in so far as it is just? Think well before you answer.

POLUS. No, Socrates, I cannot maintain that.

SOCRATES. Next take this question. Must there be corresponding to every action something which is the object of the action?

POLUS. I think so.

SOCRATES. Does what the object has done to it correspond in nature and quality to the act of the agent? For example, if a stroke is delivered something must be struck, mustn't it?

POLUS. Inevitably.

SOCRATES. And if the agent strikes violently or quickly the object must be struck in the same way?

POLUS. Yes.

SOCRATES. The effect on the object of the stroke is qualified in the same way as the act of the striker?

POLUS. Of course.

SOCRATES. Again, if there is a fire must something be burnt?

POLUS. Naturally.

SOCRATES. And if it burns violently or painfully what is burnt must be burnt in the corresponding way?

POLUS. Certainly.

SOCRATES. And does the same hold good if a cut is made? Something is cut?

POLUS. Yes.

SOCRATES. And if the cut is big or deep or painful the object cut receives a cut corresponding in kind to what the agent inflicts?

POLUS. Obviously.

SOCRATES. To sum up, do you agree with what I said a moment ago, that what the object has done to it is qualified in the same way as what the agent does?

POLUS. I agree.

SOCRATES. Then, if that is granted, is being punished active or passive?

POLUS. Passive, Socrates, of course.

SOCRATES. Then there must be a corresponding agent?

POLUS. Obviously; the man who inflicts the punishment.

SOCRATES. Does a man who punishes rightly punish justly?

POLUS. Yes.

SOCRATES. And is his action just or unjust?

POLUS. Just.

SOCRATES. Then the man who is punished for an offence is treated justly?

POLUS. Obviously.

SOCRATES. And we have agreed that what is just is fine?

POLUS. Certainly.

SOCRATES. Then the man who punishes does a fine thing, and the man who is punished has a fine thing done to him.

POLUS. Yes.

SOCRATES, And if fine, good, since it must be either pleasant or useful. 477

POLUS. Inevitably.

SOCRATES. Then the treatment received by the man who is punished is good?

POLUS. Apparently.

SOCRATES. Then it must be a benefit to him?

POLUS. Yes.

SOCRATES. And is the benefit what I take it to be, that if he is justly punished his soul is improved?

POLUS. Probably.

SOCRATES. Then the man who is punished is freed from badness of soul?

POLUS. Yes.

SOCRATES. In that case, is he not freed from the worst of all bad things? Consider; where a man's material fortune is concerned can you name any bad state except poverty?

POLUS. No.

SOCRATES. And what of his physical constitution? Doesn't a bad state here mean weakness and disease and deformity and the like?

POLUS. Yes.

SOCRATES. Now, do you recognize the existence of such a thing as a bad state of the soul?

POLUS. Of course.

SOCRATES. Do you mean by this wickedness and ignorance and cowardice and so on?

POLUS. Certainly.

SOCRATES. Then in these three things, fortune, body, and soul you recognize three corresponding bad states, poverty, disease, and wickedness?

POLUS. Yes.

SOCRATES. Now which of these three bad states is the basest? Is it not wickedness and badness of soul in general?

POLUS. Certainly.

SOCRATES. And if it is the basest is it not the worst?

POLUS. What do you mean, Socrates?

SOCRATES. Simply this. We agreed before that in any comparison of baseness the first place must be assigned to what produces either the greatest pain or the greatest harm or both.

POLUS. Agreed.

SOCRATES. And we have now agreed on the supreme baseness of wickedness and all badness of soul?

POLUS. Yes.

SOCRATES. Then its supreme baseness must be due to its being either surpassingly painful or surpassingly harmful, or both?

POLUS. It must.

SOCRATES. Now, are wickedness and excess and cowardice and ignorance more painful than poverty and sickness?

POLUS. Nothing in our discussion leads me to think so, Socrates.

SOCRATES. Then, since by your own admission badness of soul is not supremely painful, it must owe its superiority in baseness over other kinds of badness to the fact that it produces a prodigious degree of harm and evil.

POLUS. It would seem so.

SOCRATES. I suppose that what produces the greatest harm must be the greatest evil in the world?

POLUS. Yes.

SOCRATES. Then wickedness and excess and other kinds of badness of soul are the greatest evil that exists?

POLUS. That seems clear.

SOCRATES. Now, what is the art which relieves a man from poverty? Isn't it the art of making money?

POLUS. Yes.

SOCRATES. And what cures disease? Isn't it the art of medicine?

POLUS. Of course.

SOCRATES. Then what is the art which cures vice and 478 wickedness? If you are at a loss for an answer when it is put like that, look at it in this way. Where do we take sufferers from physical ailments?

POLUS. To the doctor, Socrates.

SOCRATES. And those who are wicked and licentious?

POLUS. To the judge, do you mean?

SOCRATES. To be punished?

POLUS. Yes.

SOCRATES. Do not those who punish rightly employ some kind of justice in doing so?

POLUS. Obviously.

SOCRATES. Then money-making cures poverty, medicine disease, and justice excess and wickedness.

POLUS. So it seems.

SOCRATES. Now which of these is the finest?

POLUS. Which of what?

SOCRATES. Money-making, medicine, and justice.

POLUS. Justice, Socrates, by a long way.

SOCRATES. If it is the finest, must it not produce either the greatest pleasure or the greatest benefit or both?

POLUS. Yes.

SOCRATES. Is medical treatment pleasant? Do people like being in the hands of doctors?

POLUS. Not in my opinion.

SOCRATES. But it is beneficial, isn't it?

POLUS. Yes.

SOCRATES. It relieves a man from a great trouble so that it is worth while undergoing the pain to regain one's health.

POLUS. Of course.

SOCRATES. Physically speaking, which is the happier condition, to be cured by a doctor or never to be ill at all?

POLUS. Obviously, never to be ill at all.

SOCRATES. Then happiness, it seems, consists not so much in being relieved of trouble as in never being in trouble in the first place.

POLUS. Yes.

SOCRATES. Again, if two men have a disease, whether physical or spiritual, which is the more miserable, the man who undergoes treatment and is cured of his ailment, or the man who has no treatment and continues to suffer?

POLUS. I suppose the man who has no treatment.

SOCRATES. Didn't we agree that to be punished is to be cured of the worst of all ailments, wickedness?

POLUS. Yes.

SOCRATES. Because justice is a moral physician and cures men of their excesses and makes them better people.

POLUS. Yes.

SOCRATES. Then the happiest man is the man who has no badness in his soul, since this has been shown to be the worst of all bad things.

POLUS. Clearly.

SOCRATES. And the next happiest is the man who is cured.

POLUS. Apparently.

SOCRATES. That is to say, the man who undergoes reproof and chastisement and is punished for his faults.

POLUS. Yes.

SOCRATES. And the worst life is the life of the man who continues in wickedness and is not cured.

POLUS. It appears so.

SOCRATES. But isn't he precisely the man who commits the greatest crimes and indulges in the greatest wickedness and yet manages never to undergo reproof and punishment and retribution; the man in fact who behaves just as you say Archelaus has behaved and all the other dictators and orators and potentates? 479

POLUS. So it seems.

SOCRATES. Their achievements, it would appear, my good friend, are comparable to those of a man suffering from the most serious ailments, who manages to avoid giving any account of his physical defects to the doctors and undergoing treatment, because, like a child, he is afraid of the pain involved in cautery and surgery. Don't you agree?

POLUS. Yes.

SOCRATES. Such a man is presumably ignorant of the nature of health and physical well-being. And the agreement which we have now reached, Polus, points to the conclusion that those who flee from justice are in a similar condition; they see the pain which punishment involves but are blind to its benefits and do not realize that to be chained to an unhealthy body is a far less miserable fate than the companionship of an unhealthy, rotten, wicked, impure soul. So they strain every nerve to escape punishment and to avoid being cured of the worst of all ailments; for this purpose they procure wealth and friends and make themselves as persuasive speakers as they can. But if we are right in what we have agreed, Polus, do you see what conclusions emerge from our discussion? Or would you prefer that we should sum them up?

POLUS. By all means, if you like.

SOCRATES. First, it emerges that wickedness and wicked actions are a very great evil. Do you agree?

POLUS. It seems so, at any rate.

SOCRATES. Next, has it not been demonstrated that being punished is a way of deliverance from evil?

POLUS. It looks like it.

SOCRATES. And that not being punished renders the evil permanent?

POLUS. Yes.

SOCRATES. Then acting wickedly stands only second in the list of evil things. The first and greatest of all is not to be punished for one's wicked actions.

POLUS. Apparently so.

SOCRATES. Wasn't this exactly the point at issue between us, my friend? You envied Archelaus for committing the greatest crimes with impunity, and I was of the contrary opinion and maintained that Archelaus or anyone else who escapes punishment for crime must be miserable above all other men, and that as a general rule the man who does wrong is more miserable than the man who is wronged, and the man who escapes punishment more miserable than the man who receives it. Wasn't that what I said?

POLUS. Yes.

SOCRATES. And has it not been demonstrated that I was right?

POLUS. So it appears.

480 SOCRATES. Well then, Polus, if this is true, where is the great use of oratory? Doesn't it follow from our discussion that a man's duty is to keep himself from doing wrong, because he will otherwise bring great evil upon himself?

POLUS. Certainly.

SOCRATES. And if he or anyone he cares for does wrong, he ought of his own accord to go where he will most quickly be punished, to the judge, that is, as he would to a doctor, in order that the disease of wickedness may not become chronic and cause his soul to fester till it is incurable. What else can we say, Polus, if our previous conclusions hold good? Doesn't it inevitably follow that nothing else will be consistent with them?

POLUS. There is no other possibility, Socrates.

SOCRATES. Then we shall have no use for oratory, Polus, as means of defence either for our own misdeeds or for those of our parents or friends or children or country. It may however be of service if one adopts the contrary view and holds it to be a man's duty to denounce himself in the first place for his misdeeds and next any of his family or friends who may do wrong, bringing the crime out of concealment into the light of day in order that the wrong-doer may be punished and regain his health. Such a man must force himself and others not to play the coward, but to submit to the law with closed eyes like a man, as one would to surgery or cautery, ignoring the pain for the sake of the good result which it will bring. Whatever the punishment which the crime deserves he must offer himself to it cheerfully, whether it be flogging or imprisonment or a fine or banishment or death. He must be the first to accuse himself and members of his family, and the use that he will make of oratory will be to ensure that by having their misdeeds brought to light wrong-doers are delivered from the supreme evil of wickedness. Are we to agree with that line of conduct, Polus, or not?

POLUS. It sounds extraordinary to me, Socrates, but I suppose that it is consistent with our previous discussion.

SOCRATES. Then must we not either upset the conclusions we have already reached or accept this as their necessary corollary?

POLUS. Yes, that is so.

SOCRATES. Then again, take the converse situation.[1] Suppose that it is ever right for a man to inflict injury on an enemy or on anyone else, provided of course that he runs no risk of being injured himself by the enemy – that is a point one must be on one's guard against. On that hypothesis, if the enemy injures a third party, one must clearly make every effort, both in speech and action, to prevent his being brought to book and coming before the judge at all; if that is impossible one must contrive that he gets off unpunished. If he has stolen a lot of money he must not pay it back, but keep it and spend it on himself and his family without regard to God or man; if he has committed crimes for which the penalty is death he must not be executed. The most desirable thing would be that he should never die, but live for ever in an immortality of crime; the next best that he should live as long as possible in that condition. To ensure that result, Polus, I allow that oratory might be of service, since it seems to me unlikely to be of much use to a man who is not going to do wrong. That is, supposing that it has any use at all, which it was demonstrated in our previous discussion that it has not.

CALLICLES. Tell me, Chaerephon, is Socrates in earnest about this or is he joking?

481

1. The bearing of this speech has sometimes been misunderstood. Popular Greek morality taught that right consists in doing harm to one's enemies as well as good to one's friends; this is the view put forward by Polemarchus at the beginning of the *Republic* and demolished by Socrates. Here the assumption that it can ever be right to injure one's enemy is of course ironical, and the irony is heightened by the proviso that one must run no risk of being injured oneself in the process. But, granted the assumption, the conclusion, in the light of what has been established, is sound; the perfect form of revenge is to encourage one's enemy in wrong-doing and protect him against the consequences.

CHAEREPHON. In my opinion, Callicles, he is utterly
in earnest. But there's nothing like asking himself,
if you want to know.

CALLICLES. That is exactly what I am eager to do.
Tell me, Socrates, are we to suppose that you are
joking or in earnest? If you are serious and what
you say is true, we shall have human life turned
completely upside down; we are doing, apparently,
the complete opposite of what we ought.

SOCRATES. My dear Callicles, if the feelings of every
human being were peculiar to himself and different
from those of every other human being, instead of
our possessing, for all the diversity of our experience,
something in common, it would not be easy for one
man to make his own situation clear to another. I
say this because I have noticed that you and I have
a certain fellow-feeling; we are both lovers and for
each of us his passion has a double object; I am in
love with Alcibiades the son of Cleinias and with
philosophy, you with the democracy of Athens and
with Demos the son of Pyrilampes.[1]

Now I observe whenever the occasion arises that
for all your cleverness you are unable to contradict
any assertion made by the object of your love, but
shift your ground this way and that. This happens
in the assembly; if the Athenian democracy denies
any statement made by you in a speech, you change

1. Socrates' relations with Alcibiades are described at length
in the *Symposium*. Cf. Penguin translation, pp. 96 *ff.* and Introduction, pp. 27 *ff.* If the dramatic date of the *Gorgias* is
405 B.C., the mention of Alcibiades here and at p. 135 below
constitutes a further anachronism; he had finally left Athens in
407, and in any case was far too old to be spoken of in these
terms. The same holds good for Demos, son of Pyrilampes
(cf. Introduction, p. 14), who is introduced for the sake of the
pun on his name. The point which Plato wishes to emphasize
is that a popular orator is as dependent on the whims of the
public as a lover on those of his beloved.

your policy in deference to its wishes; and the same is true of your behaviour towards that handsome young man the son of Pyrilampes. Such is your inability to oppose the wishes and statements of those you love that, if surprise were expressed at the strangeness of the things which from time to time they cause you to say, you would probably answer, if you wanted to be truthful, that unless your loves can be stopped from saying these things you will not stop talking as you do either.

482

I ask you then to be prepared to accept a similar answer from me, and not to be surprised that I speak as I do. The only remedy is to stop *my* love, philosophy, from talking like this. She is perpetually saying, my dear friend, what you are now hearing from me, and she is a great deal less capricious than my other love. The son of Cleinias never keeps to the same line for two minutes together, but philosophy never changes. It is her statements which are causing your present surprise, and you yourself were there when she made them. You must then prove her wrong, as I said just now, when she asserts that wrong-doing and not being punished for wrong-doing are the worst of all evils; otherwise, Callicles, I swear by the dog which the Egyptians worship that Callicles will never be at peace with himself; he will remain at variance with himself all his life long. Yet, I think, my good sir, that it would be better for me to have a musical instrument or a chorus which I was directing in discord and out of tune, better that the mass of mankind should disagree with me and contradict me than that I, a single individual, should be out of harmony with myself and contradict myself.

CALLICLES. Your language, Socrates, shows all the extravagance of a regular catch-penny speaker; and the reason for your present outburst of claptrap is that the very thing has happened to Polus that he blamed Gorgias for allowing to happen to him in his encounter with you. Gorgias said in answer to a question from you that if a would-be oratorical pupil came to him ignorant of the nature of right he would teach it to him, and Polus declared that this answer was dictated by false shame, because a refusal would outrage the conventional notions of society, and that it was this admission which involved Gorgias in self-contradiction, which was just the thing that you loved. On that occasion you thoroughly deserved Polus' mockery, in my opinion; but now Polus has suffered the same fate himself. I certainly don't admire him for agreeing with you that doing wrong is baser than suffering wrong; as a result of this admission he has been entangled by you in his turn and put to silence, because he was ashamed to say what he thought. The fact is, Socrates, that under pretence of pursuing the truth you are passing off upon your audience a low, popular notion of what is fine, a notion which has its foundation merely in convention and not in nature.

Generally speaking, nature and convention are inconsistent with one another; so if from a feeling of shame a man does not dare to say what he thinks he necessarily involves himself in an inconsistency. You have discovered this subtle truth and make a dishonest use of it in argument; if a man speaks the language of convention, you meet him with a question framed in the language of nature; if he uses words in their natural sense you take them in their conventional meaning. That is what has happened in this discussion of doing wrong and suffering wrong. Polus meant what is conventionally baser, and you took up his conventional use of the word as if he had intended its natural meaning. In the natural sense anything that is a greater evil is also

483

baser – in this case suffering wrong; but conventionally doing wrong is the baser of the two. The experience of suffering wrong does not happen to anyone who calls himself a man; it happens to a slave who had better die than live, seeing that when he is wronged and insulted he cannot defend himself or anyone else for whom he cares. Conventions, on the other hand, are made, in my opinion, by the weaklings who form the majority of mankind. They establish them and apportion praise and blame with an eye to themselves and their own interests, and in an endeavour to frighten those who are stronger and capable of getting the upper hand they say that ambition is base and wrong, and that wrong-doing consists in trying to gain an advantage over others; being inferior themselves, they are content, no doubt, if they can stand on an equal footing with their betters.

That is why by convention an attempt to gain an advantage over the majority is said to be wrong and base, and men call it criminal; nature, on the other hand, herself demonstrates that it is right that the better man should prevail over the worse and the stronger over the weaker. The truth of this can be seen in a variety of examples, drawn both from the animal world and from the complex communities and races of human beings; right consists in the superior ruling over the inferior and having the upper hand. By what right, for example, did Xerxes invade Greece and his father Scythia, to take two of the countless instances that present themselves?[1] My conviction is that these actions are in accordance with nature; indeed, I would go so far as to say that

1. Xerxes' invasion of Greece took place in 480 B.C. and was ended by his defeats at Salamis and Plataea. His father Darius invaded Scythia, c. 512 B.C.; the expedition, which had no lasting result, is described by Herodotus.

they are in accordance with natural law, though not perhaps with the conventional law enacted by us. Our way is to take the best and strongest among us from an early age and endeavour to mould their character as men tame lions; we subject them to a course of charms and spells and try to enslave them by repetition of the dogma that men ought to be equal and that equality is fine and right. But if there arises a man sufficiently endowed by nature, he will shake off and break through and escape from all these trammels; he will tread underfoot our texts and spells and incantations and unnatural laws, and by an act of revolt reveal himself our master instead of our slave, in the full blaze of the light of natural justice. Pindar seems to me to express the same thought as mine in the poem in which he speaks of 'Law, the king of all, men and gods alike', and goes on to say that this law 'carries things off with a high hand, making might to be right. Witness the deeds of Heracles when without paying a price ...' or words to that effect. I do not know the poem by heart, but his meaning is that Heracles drove off the oxen of Geryon without paying for them or receiving them as a gift, because this was natural justice, and that oxen and all the other possessions of those who are weaker and inferior belong to the man who is better and superior.[1]

484

That is the truth of the matter, and you will realize it if you abandon philosophy and turn to more important pursuits. Philosophy, Socrates, is a pretty toy, if one indulges in it with moderation at the right time of life; but if one pursues it further than

1. The context of this Pindaric fragment is unknown, and we cannot be sure that Callicles' interpretation of it is justified. Geryon was a giant with three bodies and three heads, whose cattle were stolen from him by Heracles in one of his most celebrated exploits.

one should it is absolute ruin. However gifted a man may be, if he studies philosophy to an advanced age he will inevitably lack all the accomplishments which one must possess if one is to be thought a gentleman and a person of consideration.

People of this sort have no knowledge of the legal code of their city, or of the principles to be employed in private or public business, or of the pleasures and passions of mankind; in a word, they are absolutely ignorant of human nature. So when they are involved in any public or private matter they are as ridiculous as I imagine men of affairs to be when they meddle with your pursuits and discussions. It comes in fact to what Euripides said:

> *Every man shines and strives for excellence*
> *In the pursuit wherein his talents lie:*
> *To this he gives the chief of all his days.*[1]

485   He will shun and depreciate what he is weak in, and exalt its opposite, out of self-love and in the belief that he is thus reflecting credit upon himself.

In my opinion, however, the best course is to have some acquaintance with both practice and theory. It is a fine thing to have a tincture of philosophy, just so much as makes an educated person, and there is no disgrace in a lad philosophizing. But when a man of maturer years remains devoted to this study the thing becomes absurd, Socrates, and I have the same feeling about philosophers as I have about those who stammer and play childish games. It is all very well for a child to talk and behave thus; I find

1. These lines, and the subsequent quotations and adaptations in this speech of Callicles, are taken from the lost *Antiope* of Euripides. This contained a scene in which Zethus and Amphion, the twin sons of Antiope and Zeus, the former a shepherd and huntsman and the latter a musician, argue the merits of the life of the man of action and the life of the artist, and each depreciates the pursuits of the other and extols his own.

it charming and delightful and quite in keeping with the tender age of a boy of spirit; in fact, when I hear a tiny boy articulating clearly I feel distaste; it offends my ear and seems to have a slavish ring about it. But when one hears a grown man stammering or sees him playing like a child it is ridiculous, and he deserves a whipping for his unmanly behaviour.

I feel just the same about students of philosophy. I like philosophy in a young lad; it is thoroughly suitable and a mark of a liberal nature; a lad who neglects philosophy I regard as mean-spirited and never likely to entertain any fine or noble ambition. But when I see an older man still at philosophy and refusing to abandon it, that man seems to me, Socrates, to need a whipping. As I said just now, such a person, however great his natural gifts, will never be a real man; shunning the busy life of the heart of the city and the meetings in which, as the poet says, 'men win renown', he will spend the rest of his life in obscurity, whispering with three or four lads in a corner and never uttering any sentiment which is large or liberal or adequate to the occasion.

Now I am very well disposed towards you, Socrates, and consequently I find myself feeling much as Zethus felt towards Amphion in the play of Euripides that I quoted a moment ago. Indeed, I am inclined to adapt what Zethus said to his brother and to say to you: 'Socrates, you are neglecting what ought to engage your attention; you choose to disguise by behaving like a boy the fine natural gifts that you were born with, and the result is that you cannot contribute a word of value to the deliberations of a court, or seize upon a plausible and convincing point, or frame a bold plan in another's cause.' Do not be offended, Socrates – I am speaking out of pure good will – if I ask you whether you aren't ashamed to be in this plight,

486

which I believe you to share with all those who plunge deeper and deeper into philosophy.

As things are now, if anyone were to arrest you or one of your sort and hale you off to prison on a charge of which you were innocent, you would be quite helpless – you can be sure of that; you would be in a daze and gape and have nothing to say, and when you got into court, however sorry a rascal the prosecutor might be, you would be condemned to death, if he chose to ask for the death penalty.

But what kind of wisdom can we call it, Socrates, that 'takes a man of parts and spoils his gifts', so that he cannot defend himself or another from mortal danger, but lets his enemies rob him of all his goods, and lives to all intents and purposes the life of an outlaw in his own city? A man like that, if you will pardon a rather blunt expression, can be slapped on the face with complete impunity.

Take my advice then, my good sir; 'abandon argument, learn the accomplishments of active life', which will give you the reputation of a man of sense. 'Leave others to dispute the niceties' of what I don't know whether to call folly or nonsense; 'their only outcome is a barren house'. Take for your models not the men who spend their time on these petty quibbles, but those who have a good livelihood and reputation and many other blessings.

SOCRATES. If my soul were made of gold, Callicles, can you imagine how happy I should be to light upon one of those touchstones by which gold is tried? I should like it to be of the best possible kind, so that if, when I tried the condition of my soul against it, the result were satisfactory, I could be perfectly confident of being in a good state and in need of no further test.

CALLICLES. What is the point of this, Socrates?

SOCRATES. I will tell you. I believe that in meeting you I have hit upon just such a lucky find.

CALLICLES. What do you mean?

SOCRATES. I am quite sure that if *you* agree with me about anything of which I am convinced in my heart we shall have there the actual truth. I have noticed that anyone who is to form a right judgement whether a soul is living well or the reverse must have three qualities, all of which you possess, understanding, good will, and readiness to be perfectly frank. I encounter many people who are not qualified to put me to the test because they are not wise like you; others are wise but unwilling to tell me the truth because they have not the same regard for me as you; and our two foreign friends, Gorgias and Polus, though they are well-disposed towards me as well as wise, are nevertheless somewhat lacking in frankness and more hampered by inhibitions than they ought to be. How far these inhibitions extend is shown by the fact that each of them has been reduced by false shame to contradict himself before a large audience and on an extremely important subject.

487

You, however, possess all those qualities which the others lack; you have had a sound education, as many Athenians would declare, and you are well-disposed towards me. If you ask what evidence I have of this, Callicles, I know that you have been a partner in philosophical discussion with Tisander of Aphidna, Andron the son of Androtion, and Nausicydes of Cholargeis,[1] and I once overheard the four of you debating how far one ought to pursue philosophy. You came to the conclusion that

1. Nothing is otherwise known of Tisander. Andron is one of the company surrounding Hippias in the *Protagoras*. Nausicydes may be the same as a wealthy grain-merchant mentioned by Xenophon in the *Memorabilia*.

one should not aim at any very exact study of it and you warned one another to be careful, for fear of finding when it was too late that you had ruined yourselves by over-education. So when I hear from you now the same advice as you gave to your most intimate friends, I have sufficient proof that you sincerely wish me well. As for your being the sort of man who speaks his mind without any sort of inhibition, the speech which you have just made is in harmony with your own assertion to that effect.

This then is how matters stand at present. Any point on which you agree with me we can regard on both sides as sufficiently established; there will be no need to apply any other test, since you will never acquiesce from lack of understanding or excess of false shame or from any desire to deceive me, since by your own account you are my friend. So then it will be no exaggeration to say that agreement between us is bound to result in absolute truth.

In spite of your reproaches, Callicles, there can be no finer subject for discussion than the question what a man should be like and what occupation he should engage in and how far he should pursue it, both in earlier and later life. If anything in the conduct of my life is amiss, be sure that this arises from ignorance on my part, not from wilfulness; so do not abandon the attempt to instruct me which you have begun, but give me a thorough demonstration what occupation I ought to follow and how I can best embark on it. And if hereafter you find that I fail to put into practice anything to which I now give my assent, set me down for a mere dolt and never waste your advice on such a good-for-nothing again.

Go back to the beginning and tell me again what you and Pindar mean by natural right. Am I mistaken in thinking that according to you right con-

488

sists in the stronger seizing the property of the weaker and the better ruling the worse and the more gifted having an advantage over the less?

CALLICLES. No; that is what I said and what I still maintain.

SOCRATES. But do you mean that 'better' and 'stronger' are the same? I couldn't quite make out your meaning on this point. Do you mean by 'stronger' those who have greater physical strength, and must the weaker obey the stronger, as you seemed to imply when you spoke of big states attacking small in accordance with natural right, because they are stronger and physically more powerful, as if 'more powerful' and 'stronger' and 'better' were synonymous terms? Is it possible to be better, but at the same time less powerful and weaker, and stronger, but also more vicious? Or are 'better' and 'stronger' to be defined as the same? This is the point on which I want a clear statement; are 'stronger' and 'better' and 'more powerful' synonymous or not?

CALLICLES. I tell you quite explicitly that they are synonymous.

SOCRATES. Now are not the mass of men naturally stronger than the individual man? And these are the people, as you said a while ago, who impose their conventional laws upon the individual.

CALLICLES. Of course.

SOCRATES. Then the laws imposed by the majority are laws imposed by the stronger.

CALLICLES. Certainly.

SOCRATES. And therefore by the better? The stronger are also the better by your account, I think.

CALLICLES. Yes.

SOCRATES. Then since they are stronger the laws which they establish are by nature good?

CALLICLES. I agree.

SOCRATES. But is it not the conventional belief of the majority, as you said yourself just now, that equality is right and that it is a baser thing to do wrong than to suffer wrong? Answer yes or no, and take care that you in your turn are not betrayed by a feeling of shame. Do the majority believe or do they not that equality, not inequality, is right, and that it is baser to do wrong than to suffer wrong? Don't grudge me an answer to this question, Callicles. If you agree with me, let me hear the point established on your authority, the authority of a man well able to distinguish truth from falsehood.

489

CALLICLES. Very well, that is the belief of the masses.

SOCRATES. Then the belief that it is baser to do wrong than to suffer wrong and that equality is right appears to be founded in nature as well as in convention. It looks as if what you said earlier were not true, and you were wrong when you accused me of knowing that convention and nature were inconsistent, and of making a dishonest use of this knowledge in argument, by taking in a conventional sense words intended by the speaker in a natural sense, and *vice versa*.

CALLICLES. There is no end to the rubbish this fellow talks. Tell me, Socrates, aren't you ashamed at your age of laying these verbal traps and counting it a god-send if a man makes a slip of the tongue? Do you really suppose that by 'stronger' I mean anything but 'better'? Haven't I already told you that they are the same? Do you take me to mean that, if you sweep together a heap of slaves and riff-raff useful only for their brawn, and they say this or that, what they say is to have the force of law?

SOCRATES. Ah! my clever friend, is that the line you take?

CALLICLES. Certainly it is.

SOCRATES. Well, my good sir, I guessed some time

ago that that or something like it was what you understood by 'stronger' and my repeating the question arises from my eagerness to grasp your precise meaning. Clearly you don't believe that two men are better than one or your slaves better than you, simply because they are physically more powerful. Tell me again from the start what you mean by 'better' if you don't mean 'more powerful'. And I must ask you, honoured sir, to be a little milder in your style of teaching; otherwise I shall run away from your school.

CALLICLES. You are pleased to be sarcastic, Socrates.

SOCRATES. No, Callicles, I am not; I swear it by Zethus, whose person you borrowed just now to utter a number of sarcasms at my expense. Come now, tell me whom you mean by 'better' men.

CALLICLES. I mean those who are more gifted.

SOCRATES. Then don't you see that you too are uttering mere words without meaning? Tell me, pray, do you mean by 'better' and 'stronger' those who are more intelligent, or something else?

CALLICLES. That is exactly what I do mean, most emphatically.

SOCRATES. Then on your theory it must often happen 490 that one wise man is stronger than ten thousand fools, and that he ought to rule over them as subjects and have the lion's share of everything. That is what you seem to mean – there is no verbal trap here, I assure you – if one man is stronger than ten thousand.

CALLICLES. That is exactly what I do mean. My belief is that natural right consists in the better and wiser man ruling over his inferiors and having the lion's share.

SOCRATES. Stop there one moment. What would you say in the following situation? Suppose a number of us were collected in the same spot, as we are now, with plenty of food and drink between us, a heterogeneous crowd of strong and weak together, but containing one man wiser than the rest of us about such matters by virtue of his medical knowledge. And suppose that this man, as is quite likely, were physically more powerful than some but less powerful than other members of the crowd. Should we say that for the present purpose the doctor, being wiser than we, is also better and stronger?

CALLICLES. Certainly.

SOCRATES. Is he then to have more of the food than we because he is better, or is his authority over us to be shown by his being in control of the distribution? If he is not to suffer for it, he will not appropriate the largest ration for his personal consumption; he will have more than some and less than others, and if he happens to be the greatest invalid of the party the best man will get the smallest share. Isn't that how it will be, Callicles?

CALLICLES. You talk of food and drink and doctors and nonsense of that sort. That is not what I am referring to.

SOCRATES. Then do you maintain that the wiser man is also the better? Yes or no.

CALLICLES. Yes.

SOCRATES. And that the better man ought to have the larger share?

CALLICLES. Yes, but not of food and drink.

SOCRATES. Very well; perhaps you mean of clothes, and the best weaver ought to have the biggest coat, and go about the town in more and finer clothes than other people.

CALLICLES. Clothes, forsooth!

SOCRATES. As for shoes, obviously the man who is best and wisest about them will have the advantage there; the shoemaker will walk about in the largest shoes and have the greatest number of them.

CALLICLES. Shoes indeed! Bosh!

SOCRATES. If you don't mean that sort of thing, perhaps you mean, for example, that a farmer, who is intelligent and a fine fellow where land is concerned, should have a larger share of seed than other people, and use the greatest possible quantity of seed on his own farm.

CALLICLES. Still the same stale old language, Socrates.

SOCRATES. Yes, Callicles, and on the same subjects.

CALLICLES. You simply never stop talking of cob- 491 blers and fullers and cooks and doctors; as if our argument were concerned with them!

SOCRATES. Then kindly tell me in what sphere a man must show his greater strength and intelligence in order to establish a right to an advantage over others. Or are you going to refuse to entertain any of my suggestions, and at the same time make none of your own?

CALLICLES. I have told you already what I mean, Socrates. First of all, when I speak of 'stronger' I don't mean cobblers or cooks; I mean people with the intelligence to know how political matters should be handled, and not only intelligence but courage; people who have the ability to carry out their ideas, and who will not shrink from doing so through faintness of heart.

SOCRATES. Do you notice, my dear Callicles, how you and I find fault with one another for quite different reasons? You blame me for constantly using the same language, while I, on the contrary, find it a defect in you that you never keep to the same line about the same subject. At one moment you defined the better and stronger as the more powerful; next as the more intelligent; and now you come out with yet another idea; you say that the better and stronger are a braver sort of people. Tell us my good friend, and be done with it, what you mean by the better and stronger and how they differ from other people.

CALLICLES. I have told you that I mean people who are intelligent in political matters and have the courage of their convictions. They are the people who ought to rule states, and right consists in them as rulers having an advantage over the rest, who are their subjects.

SOCRATES. Tell me, will they be rulers of themselves?

CALLICLES. What do you mean?

SOCRATES. I mean each man being master of himself. Or is there no need for self-mastery as long as one is master of others?

CALLICLES. What do you mean by self-mastery?

SOCRATES. Nothing in the least recondite. I use the word simply in the popular sense, of being moderate and in control of oneself and master of one's own passions and appetites.

CALLICLES. What a funny fellow you are, Socrates. The people that you call moderate are the half-witted.

SOCRATES. How so? Anybody can see that I don't mean them.

CALLICLES. Oh! but you do, Socrates. For how can a man be happy that is in subjection to anyone whatever? I tell you frankly that natural good and right consist in this, that the man who is going to live as a man ought should encourage his appetites to be as strong as possible instead of repressing them, and be able by means of his courage and intelligence to satisfy them in all their intensity by providing them with whatever they happen to desire.

For the majority, I know, this is an impossible ideal; that is why, in an endeavour to conceal their own weakness, they blame the minority whom they are ashamed of not being able to imitate, and maintain that excess is a disgraceful thing. As I said before, they try to make slaves of men of better

492

natural gifts, and because through their own lack of manliness they are unable to satisfy their passions they praise moderation and righteousness. To those who are either of princely birth to begin with or able by their own qualities to win office or absolute rule or power what could in truth be more disgraceful or injurious than moderation, which involves their voluntary subjection to the conventions and standards and criticism of the majority, when they might enjoy every advantage without interference from anybody? How can they fail to be wretched when they are prevented by your fine righteousness and moderation from favouring their friends at the expense of their enemies, even when they are rulers in their own city?

The truth, Socrates, which you profess to be in search of is in fact this; luxury and excess and licence, provided that they can obtain sufficient backing, are virtue and happiness; all the rest is mere flummery, unnatural conventions of society, worthless cant.

SOCRATES. Your frank statement of your position, Callicles, certainly does not lack spirit. You set out plainly in the light of day opinions which other people entertain but are loth to express. Don't weaken at all, I beseeech you, so that we may come to a clear conclusion how life should be lived. And tell me this. You maintain, do you not, that if a man is to be what he ought he should not repress his appetites but let them grow as strong as possible and satisfy them by any means in his power, and that such behaviour is virtue?

CALLICLES. Yes, I do.

SOCRATES. Then the view that those who have no wants are happy is wrong?

CALLICLES. Of course; at that rate stones and corpses would be supremely happy.

SOCRATES. Nevertheless even the life which you describe has its alarming side. I should not wonder if Euripides may not be right when he says:

Who knows if life be death or death be life?[1]

493 and if perhaps it may not be we who are in fact dead. This is a view that I have heard maintained before now by one of the pundits, who declares that we in our present condition are dead. Our body is the tomb in which we are buried,[2] and the part of the soul in which our appetites reside is liable by reason of its gullibility to be carried in the most contrary directions. This same part, because of its instability and readiness to be influenced, a witty man, Sicilian perhaps or Italian, has by a play upon words allegorically called a pitcher. In the same vein he labels fools 'uninitiated' (or 'leaky'), and that part of their soul which contains the appetites, which is intemperate and as it were the reverse of watertight, he represents as a pitcher with holes in it, because it cannot be filled up. Thus in direct opposition to you, Callicles, he maintains that of all the inhabitants of Hades – meaning by Hades the invisible world – the uninitiated are the most wretched, being engaged in pouring water into a leaky pitcher out of an equally leaky sieve. The sieve, according to my informant, he uses as an image of the soul, and his motive for comparing the souls of fools to sieves is that they are leaky and unable to retain their contents on account of their fickle and forgetful nature.[3]

1. A fragment of the *Polyidus*, parodied by Aristophanes in the *Frogs*.

2. The idea that the body (*soma*) is a tomb (*sema*) in which the immortal soul is buried is characteristic both of the Pythagorean philosophy and of the Orphic mystery religion with which Pythagoreanism had much in common. Both had considerable influence on Plato.

3. 'Sicilian' probably refers to Empedocles, who shared the view that the soul falls at birth into a state from which it must

This comparison is, no doubt, more or less grotesque, but it demonstrates the point which I want to prove to you, in order to persuade you, if I can, to change your mind, and, instead of a life of intemperate craving which can never be satisfied, to choose a temperate life which is content with whatever comes to hand and asks no more.

Does what I say influence you at all towards a conviction that the temperate are happier than the intemperate, or will any number of such allegories fail to convert you?

CALLICLES. The latter is nearer the truth, Socrates.

SOCRATES. Well, let me produce another simile from the same school as the first. Suppose that the two lives, the temperate and the intemperate, are typified by two men, each of whom has a number of casks. The casks of the first are sound and full, one of wine, one of honey, one of milk, and so on, but the supply of each of these commodities is scanty and he can procure them only with very great difficulty. This man, when once he has filled his casks, will not need to increase his store and give himself any further concern about it; as far as this matter goes his mind will be at rest. Now take the second man. He, like the first, can obtain a supply, though

---

free itself. 'Italian' almost certainly means 'Pythagorean'. The sense of the passage partly depends upon plays upon words which cannot be rendered in translation. The appetitive part of the soul is called a pitcher (*pithos*) because it is readily influenced (*pithanos*); the word for 'uninitiated' (*amyetos*) is made by a fanciful derivation to bear the secondary sense of 'leaky'; Hades is equated with *aeides*, invisible. The object of initiation is to secure the welfare of the soul in the next world, and the symbol of the leaky pitcher recalls the fate of the daughters of Danaus, whose punishment in Hades is to pour water for ever into leaky vessels. The idea that life may be death is perhaps to be interpreted in the light of this allusion; in our world an analogue to the Danaids is to be found in the behaviour of the intemperate, who may therefore be thought of as being already in Hades.

PLATO

only with difficulty; but his vessels are leaky and
rotten, so that if he is to avoid the extremity of
494   privation he must be perpetually filling them, day
and night. If such is the condition of the two lives
respectively, can you say that the life of the intemperate man is happier than the life of the temperate?
Am I making any progress towards making you
admit that the temperate life is better than the intemperate, or not?

CALLICLES. No, Socrates, you are not. The man who
has filled his casks no longer has any pleasure left.
It is just as I said a moment ago; once his casks are
filled his existence is the existence of a stone, exempt
alike from enjoyment and pain. But the pleasure of
life consists precisely in this, that there should be
as much running in as possible?

SOCRATES. But if much is to run in much must
necessarily run out, and there must be large holes
for it to escape by.

CALLICLES. Certainly.

SOCRATES. Then the existence which you are des-
cribing, so far from being that of a stone or a corpse,
is the existence of a greedy and dirty bird.[1] Tell me
now; are you speaking of such things as being
hungry and eating when one is hungry?

CALLICLES. Yes.

SOCRATES. And of being thirsty and drinking when
one is thirsty?

CALLICLES. Certainly, and of having all the other
appetites and being able to satisfy them with enjoyment. That is the happy life.

SOCRATES. Excellent, my good sir. Only you must
stick to your point and not give way out of shame.
No more must I, for that matter, it seems. Tell me

[1]. The bird in question (*charadrios*) is perhaps some species of
plover. It is said by an ancient commentator to excrete while it
eats; hence the allusion here.

first of all; can a man who itches and wants to scratch and whose opportunities of scratching are unbounded be said to lead a happy life continually scratching?

CALLICLES. How fantastic you are, Socrates, and how thoroughly vulgar.

SOCRATES. That, Callicles, is why I shocked Polus and Gorgias and made them feel shame. But you are a brave man, and will never give way to such emotions. Just answer me.

CALLICLES. Then I say that even the man who scratches lives a pleasant life.

SOCRATES. And if pleasant then happy?

CALLICLES. Of course.

SOCRATES. But suppose that the itch were not confined to his head. Must I go on with my questions? Consider what answer you will make, Callicles, if you are asked all the questions which are corollaries of this. To bring the matter to a head, take the life of a catamite; is not that dreadful and shameful and wretched? Or will you dare to say that such people are happy provided that they have an abundant supply of what they want?

CALLICLES. Aren't you ashamed to introduce such subjects into the discussion, Socrates?

SOCRATES. Who is responsible for their introduction, my fine sir? I or the person who maintains without qualification that those who feel enjoyment of whatever kind are happy, and who does not distinguish between good and bad pleasures? Tell me once more; do you declare that pleasure is identical with good, or are there some pleasures which are not good?

CALLICLES. To say that they are different would involve me in an inconsistency. I declare that they are identical.

SOCRATES. If you say what you do not think,

Callicles, you are destroying the force of your first speech, and I can no longer accept you as a satisfactory ally in my attempt to discover the truth.

CALLICLES. But you are doing just the same Socrates.

SOCRATES. If I am, I am wrong, and so are you. Can it be, my good friend, that good is not identical with enjoyment of whatever kind? Otherwise many shameful consequences will ensue besides those at which I have just hinted.

CALLICLES. That is what *you* think, Socrates.

SOCRATES. Do you really persist, Callicles, in what you affirm?

CALLICLES. Yes, I do.

SOCRATES. Shall we then continue the argument on the assumption that you are serious?

CALLICLES. By all means.

SOCRATES. Very well then; if that is your decision, solve this problem. You recognize the existence of something called knowledge, I presume?

CALLICLES. Yes.

SOCRATES. You were speaking just now, were you not, of courage existing together with knowledge?[1]

CALLICLES. I was.

SOCRATES. Meaning, I suppose, that courage and knowledge are two different things.

CALLICLES. Undoubtedly.

SOCRATES. Now then; would you call pleasure and knowledge the same or different?

CALLICLES. Different, of course, my wiseacre.

SOCRATES. And courage different from pleasure?

CALLICLES. Naturally.

SOCRATES. We must make a note of this. 'Callicles of Acharnae declared that pleasure and good are the same, but knowledge and courage are different from one another and different from good.'

1. Cf. above, p. 89.

CALLICLES. 'But Socrates of Alopece does not agree with him', or does he?

SOCRATES. He does not. Nor, I think, will Callicles, when he has examined himself properly. Tell me; do you not think that the fortunate are in the opposite state to the unfortunate?

CALLICLES. Yes.

SOCRATES. Then, if these states are opposite, is not the same true of them as of health and sickness? A man, I presume, is never both well and sick at the same time, and never ceases to be well and sick at the same time.

CALLICLES. What do you mean?

SOCRATES. Take any part of the body you like by itself; suppose a man has a malady of the eyes, what is called ophthalmia.

496

CALLICLES. Very well.

SOCRATES. He does not, I presume, enjoy health in his eyes at the same time?

CALLICLES. By no manner of means.

SOCRATES. Now, when he loses his ophthalmia, does he at that moment lose health in his eyes, so that he ends by losing both together?

CALLICLES. Certainly not.

SOCRATES. Such a conclusion would be illogical as well as surprising, wouldn't it?

CALLICLES. It would indeed.

SOCRATES. The truth is, I imagine, that he acquires and loses each condition by turns.

CALLICLES. I agree.

SOCRATES. Is the same true of strength and weakness?

CALLICLES. Yes.

SOCRATES. And of quickness and slowness?

CALLICLES. Of course.

SOCRATES. Now take good and happiness and their opposites, evil and misery; are both of these acquired by turns and lost by turns?

CALLICLES. Unquestionably.

SOCRATES. Then, if we find any pair of things that a man loses together and possesses together those things will not be good and evil. Are we agreed about this? Think well before you answer.

CALLICLES. I agree most emphatically.

SOCRATES. Go back now to what we agreed before. Did you say that hunger was pleasant or painful? I mean just hunger by itself.

CALLICLES. I should call that painful; but to eat when one is hungry is pleasant.

SOCRATES. I understand. Still, hunger in itself is painful, is it not?

CALLICLES. Yes.

SOCRATES. And thirst also?

CALLICLES. Certainly.

SOCRATES. Shall I go on with further questions, or do you agree that every state of want and desire is painful?

CALLICLES. You need not labour the point. I agree.

SOCRATES. Very well. But drinking when one is thirsty you would call pleasant, wouldn't you?

CALLICLES. Yes.

SOCRATES. When you say 'drinking when one is thirsty', 'thirsty' is equivalent to 'in pain', is it not?

CALLICLES. Yes.

SOCRATES. And drinking is the satisfaction of the want and a pleasure?

CALLICLES. Yes.

SOCRATES. So it is in connexion with drinking that you speak of enjoyment?

CALLICLES. Certainly.

SOCRATES. When one is thirsty?

CALLICLES. Yes.

SOCRATES. And therefore in pain?

CALLICLES. Yes.

SOCRATES. Do you see what follows? When you

speak of drinking, when one is thirsty, you imply the experience of pleasure and pain together.[1] Can you say that these sensations don't occur together at the same time and in the same part of something which you may equally well, I think, call body or soul? Is this true or not?

CALLICLES. Quite true.

SOCRATES. Yet you say that it is impossible to be fortunate and unfortunate at the same time.

CALLICLES. I do.

SOCRATES. But you have agreed that it is possible to feel enjoyment when one is in pain.   497

CALLICLES. So it appears.

SOCRATES. Then enjoyment is not the same as good fortune nor pain as bad fortune, and pleasure is a different thing from good.

CALLICLES. I don't understand your quibbles, Socrates.

SOCRATES. Oh yes, you do, Callicles; only it suits you to feign ignorance. Just carry the argument a little further.

CALLICLES. What is the point of continuing this nonsense?

SOCRATES. To show you how clever you are, my self-appointed instructor. Is it not true that at the moment when each of us ceases to feel thirst he ceases also to feel the pleasure of drinking?

CALLICLES. I don't know what you mean.

GORGIAS. Never mind, Callicles; answer to please us as well as Socrates, so that the argument can be brought to an end.

1. This argument from the co-existence of pleasure and pain is examined more profoundly in the *Philebus*, one of the latest of the Platonic dialogues. There a distinction is drawn between 'mixed' pleasures, which involve the satisfaction of a painful want, and 'pure' pleasures, such as those of the intellect or of the aesthetic sense. The argument of the *Gorgias*, which treats all pleasure as 'mixed', is clearly unsatisfactory.

CALLICLES. But Socrates is always the same, Gorgias. He catches one out by such trivial and footling questions.

GORGIAS. What does that matter to you? It is not your reputation that will suffer. Allow Socrates to conduct the argument in his own way.

CALLICLES. Well, go on with your fiddling little questions, since Gorgias will have it so.

SOCRATES. You are lucky, Callicles, to have been initiated into the Greater Mysteries before the Lesser; I didn't think that it was allowed.[1] Go on where you left off, and tell me whether thirst and pleasure don't come to an end together for us all.

CALLICLES. Yes, they do.

SOCRATES. And the same with hunger and the other appetites? Does not the pleasure of satisfying them cease at the same moment as the desire?

CALLICLES. True.

SOCRATES. Then pains and pleasures come to an end together?

CALLICLES. Yes.

SOCRATES. But, as you agreed, good and evil do not come to an end together. Or do you wish to retract that admission?

CALLICLES. By no means. What then?

SOCRATES. The conclusion is, my friend, that good is not identical with pleasure nor evil with pain. The one pair of contraries comes to an end together and the other does not, because they are different. How then can pleasure possibly be the same as good or pain as evil? Look at the matter in another way if

1. The reference is to the Eleusinian Mysteries. An interval had to elapse between the preliminary rite at Athens (the Lesser Mysteries) and initiation proper at Eleusis (the Greater Mysteries). Socrates' sarcasm is aimed at Callicles' contempt for the preliminary dialectical steps on which any sound conclusion must be based.

you like; the conclusion will still, I think, be at variance with yours. When you call people good, you imply, do you not, the presence of good in them, in the same way as you call those in whom beauty is present beautiful?

CALLICLES. Yes.

SOCRATES. Well, do you call fools and cowards good? You didn't a while ago; you reserved the term for the brave and intelligent. They are the people you call good, aren't they?

CALLICLES. Certainly.

SOCRATES. Well, have you ever seen a foolish child enjoying itself?

CALLICLES. Yes.

SOCRATES. And for that matter a foolish man enjoying himself? 498

CALLICLES. I suppose so. But what is the point of this?

SOCRATES. Never mind; just answer.

CALLICLES. Yes, then.

SOCRATES. Have you seen an intelligent man feeling pain or pleasure?

CALLICLES. Yes.

SOCRATES. Well, which class feels greater pain or pleasure, the fools or the wise men?

CALLICLES. I don't know that there is much in it.

SOCRATES. That is enough for my purpose. Now, have you seen a coward in war?

CALLICLES. Of course.

SOCRATES. And when the enemy retreated which did you think felt greater joy, the cowards or the brave men?

CALLICLES. Greater joy? Both, as far as I could see. Anyhow, the difference was trifling.

SOCRATES. No matter for that. At any rate cowards feel joy as well as the brave?

CALLICLES. Undoubtedly.

SOCRATES. And fools too, it seems.

CALLICLES. Yes.

SOCRATES. But when the enemy advances, is pain confined to cowards, or do the brave feel it too?

CALLICLES. Both feel it.

SOCRATES. Equally?

CALLICLES. Perhaps cowards feel it more.

SOCRATES. And don't they feel greater joy when the enemy retreats?

CALLICLES. Perhaps.

SOCRATES. Then by your account pain and joy are felt in practically the same degree by fools and wise men, cowards and heroes, but if anything more keenly by cowards than by brave men?

CALLICLES. Yes.

SOCRATES. Yet the wise and brave are good, and cowards and fools bad?

CALLICLES. Yes.

SOCRATES. Then good and bad feel joy and pain in about the same degree?

CALLICLES. Yes.

SOCRATES. In that case are we to conclude that there is very little to choose in goodness and badness between the good and the bad, or even that the bad are somewhat better than the good?

CALLICLES. I simply do not know what you mean.

SOCRATES. Don't you remember that you are maintaining that the good owe their goodness to the presence in them of good, and the bad their badness to the presence of evil, and that good is identical with pleasure and evil with pain?

CALLICLES. Yes.

SOCRATES. Doesn't the sensation of joy involve the presence of pleasure or good in those who experience it?

CALLICLES. Of course.

SOCRATES. Then since good is present in them, those who feel joy are good?

CALLICLES. Yes.

SOCRATES. Again, is not pain or evil present in those who suffer pain?

CALLICLES. It is.

SOCRATES. And you say that the bad owe their badness to the presence of evil in them. Or do you retract that?

CALLICLES. No, I affirm it.

SOCRATES. Then whoever feels joy is good and whoever feels pain is bad?

CALLICLES. Certainly.

SOCRATES. And people are more or less or equally good or bad according as their experience of joy is more or less or equally intense?

CALLICLES. Yes.

SOCRATES. You say, I think, that joy and pain are felt in almost equal degree by wise men and fools, cowards and heroes, or possibly somewhat more keenly by cowards?

CALLICLES. Yes.

SOCRATES. Now give me your help in drawing the conclusion that emerges from what we have agreed. It is good to repeat and contemplate fine things two 499 or three times, they say. We affirm that a wise and brave man is good, don't we?

CALLICLES. Yes.

SOCRATES. And a fool and a coward bad?

CALLICLES. Certainly.

SOCRATES. But a man who feels joy is good?

CALLICLES. Yes.

SOCRATES. And a man who feels pain bad?

CALLICLES. Inevitably.

SOCRATES. And the good and bad feel pain and joy alike, but the bad perhaps more keenly?

CALLICLES. Yes.

SOCRATES. Then the bad man is as good and as bad as the good, or perhaps rather better. Isn't this the conclusion that follows from our premises, if one begins by equating pleasure and good? Is there any escape from it, Callicles?

CALLICLES. I've been listening to you and expressing agreement for a long time, Socrates, with the thought in my mind all along that if one gives in to you on any point even in jest, you seize on the admission triumphantly with all the eagerness of a child. As if you didn't know that like everybody else I distinguish between better and worse pleasures.[1]

SOCRATES. Come, come, Callicles, what a cheat you are. You are treating me like a child, changing your ground from moment to moment, in order to mislead me. When we began I never supposed that you would wilfully mislead me, because I thought that you were my friend. But now it appears that I was mistaken in you, and I suppose that I must make the best of it, as the saying goes, and do what I can with what you choose to give me.

What you are now saying, apparently, is that some pleasures are good and some bad. Is that right?

CALLICLES. Yes.

SOCRATES. Are good pleasures those which bring benefit and bad pleasures those which bring harm?

CALLICLES. Of course.

SOCRATES. And the beneficial are those which produce some good result, and the harmful those which produce the reverse?

CALLICLES. Yes.

SOCRATES. Do you mean the sort of pleasures we were speaking of before, the physical pleasures of eating

[1]. The sudden abandonment by Callicles of his contention that pleasure and good are identical and his admission of degrees of value in pleasure enable Socrates to recur to his criticism of oratory, which has been in abeyance since p. 48.

and drinking, for example? Are we to regard those which produce bodily health or strength or some other desirable physical quality as good and those which have the opposite effect as bad?

CALLICLES. Certainly.

SOCRATES. And does the same apply to pains? Are some good and some bad?

CALLICLES. Naturally.

SOCRATES. Then we must prefer to embrace the good of both kinds, pains as well as pleasures?

CALLICLES. By all means.

SOCRATES. And reject the bad?

CALLICLES. Obviously.

SOCRATES. If you remember, Polus and I agreed that all actions should be performed as a means to the good. Do you also agree with this, that good is the object of all actions, and that all that we do should be a means to the good, and not *vice versa*? Are you prepared to add your vote to our two?　　　　500

CALLICLES. Yes, I am.

SOCRATES. Then it follows that we should embrace pleasure among other things as a means to good, and not good as a means to pleasure.

CALLICLES. Certainly.

SOCRATES. Can *anybody* distinguish between good and bad pleasures, or does it need an expert in every particular department?

CALLICLES. It needs an expert.

SOCRATES. Then let us go back once more to what I was saying to Polus and Gorgias. I maintained, if you remember, that there are some occupations which confine themselves to the production of pleasure without making any distinction between better and worse, and others which are based on a knowledge of good and bad. I classed cookery as a knack rather than an art among the occupations which are concerned merely with pleasure, and the art of medicine among those which are concerned with good.

For friendship's sake, Callicles, I beg you not to suppose that this is a matter which calls for jesting on your part. Do not answer at random contrary to your real opinion; believe me, I am perfectly serious in what I am saying. The subject we are discussing is one which cannot fail to engage the earnest attention even of a man of small intelligence; it is nothing less than how a man should live. Is he to adopt the life to which you invite me, doing what you call a man's work, speaking in the assembly and practising oratory and engaging in politics on the principles at present in fashion among you politicians, or should he follow my example and lead the life of a philosopher; and in what is the latter life superior to the former?

Perhaps the best course is to try to distinguish them, as I did a while ago, and when we have agreed, if we can, that these two lives really are distinct, to examine how they differ from one another and which is to be preferred. But possibly you have not yet grasped my meaning?

CALLICLES. I cannot say that I have.

SOCRATES. I will put it more clearly. Since you and I have agreed that there is such a thing as good and such a thing as pleasure, and that pleasure is different from good, and that there is a particular method to be practised in the acquisition of each, in the pursuit of pleasure and in the pursuit of good – but tell me first of all whether you agree with me on this point. Do you?

CALLICLES. Yes.

SOCRATES. Well then, let me have your assent also to what I was saying to Gorgias and Polus, if it struck you at the time as being true. I was saying that in my opinion cookery, unlike medicine, is a knack, not an art, and I added that, whereas medicine studies the nature of the patient before it treats him 501 and knows the reasons which dictate its actions and can give a rational account of both, cookery on the other hand approaches in a thoroughly unmethodical way even that pleasure which is the sole object of its ministrations; it makes no study of the nature of pleasure or of the causes which produce it, but with practically no attempt at rational calculation is content to record as a matter of routine and experience what normally occurs, and is enabled to purvey its pleasures by this means.

Make up your mind then first of all whether this seems to you a satisfactory account of the matter, and whether the activities concerned with the soul may not be classified in a similar way, some of them proceeding from a scientific basis and keeping constantly in view the welfare of the soul, while others neglect this and devote themselves entirely, like cookery in the other case, to the question how to produce pleasure for the soul, without drawing any distinction between better and worse pleasures or concerning themselves in the slightest degree with anything except the giving of gratification by any means, good or bad. I think, Callicles, that there are such activities, and I call everything of this sort pandering, whether it is concerned with the body or the soul or with anything else to which its aim is to give pleasure without any regard for what is better or worse. Do you acquiesce in my opinion about this or do you reject it?

CALLICLES. Not I, Socrates; I am quite ready to agree with you, in order to bring the discussion to a close and to oblige Gorgias.

SOCRATES. And is this pandering confined to a single soul, or can it be exercised on two or more?

CALLICLES. Clearly on two or more.

SOCRATES. Then it is quite possible to pander to the souls of a crowd, without regard to its real interest?

CALLICLES. Perfectly possible, in my opinion.

SOCRATES. Can you tell what are the activities which do this? Or, if you prefer, say yes or no as I enumerate them. Take flute-playing first. Do you regard this as an activity which aims only at giving us pleasure, regardless of other considerations?

CALLICLES. Yes.

SOCRATES. And would you say the same of all kindred activities, playing the lyre at public competitions, for example?[1]

CALLICLES. Yes.

SOCRATES. What about the training of choruses and dithyrambic poetry?[2] Would you put them in the same class? Do you suppose that Cinesias the son of Meles[3] worries whether his poetry is likely to improve his hearers, or only whether it will gratify the mass of the audience?

CALLICLES. Obviously the latter, Socrates, in the case of Cinesias.

SOCRATES. Again, take his father Meles; did he aim at edification in his songs? Or even, for that matter, at giving pleasure? His voice was agony to an audience. But, leaving that aside, don't you agree

502

1. Plato held strong views on the moral effect of various sorts of music, which he treats at length in *Republic III*. The flute is enervating and demoralizing; the lyre, on the other hand, may be made a useful vehicle of education, of which it formed at Athens a recognized part; it is only lyre-playing at public competitions which is to be reprobated.

2. Here again it is not all choral poetry which is condemned, but only the production and performance of dithyrambs at the festivals of Dionysus.

3. Cinesias is ridiculed by Aristophanes for the wildness and incoherence of his dithyrambs and for their immoral tone. A fragment of the comic poet Pherecrates describes Meles as the worst performer to the lyre in the world.

that singing to the lyre and dithyrambic poetry in general were invented to give pleasure?

CALLICLES. Yes.

SOCRATES. What of the solemn and reverend Muse of tragedy? Is it the object of her earnest endeavour simply to gratify the spectators, or does she strive to avoid anything that would harm them, however pleasant and attractive, and make it her business in dialogue and song to impart wholesome but unpalatable truths, whether the audience like it or not? For which of these purposes do you suppose that tragic poetry is adapted?

CALLICLES. Obviously, Socrates, for the purpose of giving pleasure and gratifying the audience.

SOCRATES. Just what we declared a moment ago to be pandering, Callicles?

CALLICLES. No doubt.

SOCRATES. Now if one were to strip poetry of music, rhythm, and metre, what is left would be mere words, would it not?

CALLICLES. Of course.

SOCRATES. And words addressed to a large popular audience?

CALLICLES. Yes.

SOCRATES. Then poetry is a sort of public speaking?

CALLICLES. So it seems.

SOCRATES. In that case it will partake of the nature of oratory. Don't you think that the tragic poets play the part of orators in their own world of the theatre?

CALLICLES. Yes.

SOCRATES. So now between us we have discovered a sort of oratory addressed to a heterogeneous popular audience of men, women, and children, slaves as well as free men; and oratory moreover of a kind which we don't much admire, seeing that by our account of the matter it is a species of pandering.

CALLICLES. I agree.

SOCRATES. Good. Now what are we to think of the oratory addressed to the Athenian democracy and to the democratic assemblies of free men in other cities? Do the speakers in your opinion make it the constant aim of their speeches to improve their fellow-citizens as much as possible, or do they too set out merely to gratify their hearers, sacrificing the public interest to their own personal success, and treating their audience like children, whom their

503   only object is to please, without caring whether the effect of their speeches is improving or the reverse?

CALLICLES. There is no simple answer to this question as there was to the other. Some speakers are moved by a regard for the public interest, and some are such as you describe.

SOCRATES. I am content with that answer. Granted that there are two kinds of political oratory, one of them is pandering and base clap-trap; only the other is good, which aims at the edification of the souls of the citizens and is always striving to say what is best, whether it be welcome or unwelcome to the ears of the audience. But I don't believe that you have ever experienced the second type; if you can point to any orator who conforms to it, lose no time in letting me into the secret of his identity.

CALLICLES. As a matter of fact, I can't point to anyone of this kind among living speakers.

SOCRATES. Well, is there anyone that you can name among the politicians of the past, from whose first public appearance one can date a change for the better in the character of the Athenians? I don't know of any.

CALLICLES. Surely you have heard of the merits of Themistocles and Cimon and Miltiades and Pericles?

The last died not so long ago,[1] and you have heard him speak yourself.

SOCRATES. If, as you began by saying, Callicles, true virtue consists in satisfying all the desires of oneself and others, you are right; but if, as we found ourselves driven to admit in our subsequent discussion, it consists in fulfilling those desires whose satisfaction makes a man better and denying those which make him worse, and if this is a matter of expert knowledge, can you point to any of these men who comes up to this standard?

CALLICLES. I do not know how to answer you.

SOCRATES. You will find an answer, if you look carefully. Let us consider quite calmly whether any of the men you have named was of this type. Come now, the good man, who always aims at the best in what he says, will have some definite object in view, will he not? He will no more proceed at random than other professional men, each of whom chooses and employs means and materials with an eye to his particular task, in order that what he is fashioning may have a definite form. Take, for example, painters, architects, shipwrights, any other profession you like, and see how each of them arranges the different elements of his work in a certain order, and makes one part fit and harmonize with another until the thing emerges a consistent and organized whole. Among other professional men are those who deal with the body, trainers and doctors, whom we have already mentioned; they may be presumed to give order and proportion to the body. Are you prepared to give me your agreement on this point?

CALLICLES. Granted.

SOCRATES. Then whether a house is a good or bad

504

---

1. Cf. Introduction, p. 14.

house will depend on whether it is built in accordance with order and proportion or not?

CALLICLES. Yes.

SOCRATES. And the same is true of a ship?

CALLICLES. Yes.

SOCRATES. And also of our bodies?

CALLICLES. Certainly.

SOCRATES. What about the soul? Will the goodness of a soul consist in disorder or rather in a certain order and proportion?

CALLICLES. In the latter inevitably, if we are to be consistent.

SOCRATES. Now what do we call the quality which order and proportion give to the body?

CALLICLES. I suppose you mean health and strength?

SOCRATES. Exactly so. And what is the quality which order and proportion create in the soul? Try to find a name for this, like the other.

CALLICLES. Why don't you answer your own question, Socrates?

SOCRATES. I will, if you prefer it. But you must tell me whether you think I am right, and, if you don't, challenge me and not let the matter pass. In my opinion 'healthy' is the name given to the means which produce order in the body, and their result is health and every other physical excellence. Is this so or not?

CALLICLES. It is so.

SOCRATES. And the means which produce order and proportion in the soul are called 'regulation' and 'law'; these are what make men law-abiding and orderly, and so we have righteousness and moderation. Agreed?

CALLICLES. Very well.

SOCRATES. Then the good orator, being also a man of expert knowledge, will have these ends in view in any speech or action by which he seeks to influence the souls of men, in any gift which he may confer, and in any privation which he may inflict; his attention will be wholly concentrated on bringing righteousness and moderation and every other virtue to birth in the souls of his fellow-citizens, and on removing their opposites, unrighteousness and excess and vice. Do you agree?

CALLICLES. Yes.

SOCRATES. What point is there, Callicles, in administering abundance of the most delicious food and drink or any other pleasure to an ailing and miserable body, when these will often do no more good than abstinence, or even, if the matter be rightly considered, positively less? Isn't that true?

CALLICLES. Assume it to be so, by all means. 505

SOCRATES. It does a man no good, in my opinion, to live with his body in misery; the inevitable outcome is a miserable life. Don't you agree?

CALLICLES. Yes.

SOCRATES. As far as satisfying one's appetites is concerned, eating when one is hungry or drinking when one is thirsty, for example, this is generally allowed by doctors to a person in health, but an invalid is practically never permitted to have his fill of what he desires. Isn't that your experience?

CALLICLES. Yes.

SOCRATES. And is it not the same, my good sir, with the soul? As long as it is in a bad state, from ignorance and excess and unrighteousness and impiety, it must be restrained from satisfying its appetites and prevented from doing anything but what will improve it. Do you agree?

CALLICLES. Yes.

SOCRATES. Such a course is in the soul's own interest, is it not?

CALLICLES. Certainly.

SOCRATES. Isn't keeping a man from what he desires the same thing as correcting him?

CALLICLES. Yes.

SOCRATES. Then correction is better for the soul than absence of restraint, which you declared at an earlier stage to be the ideal.

CALLICLES. I don't know what you mean, Socrates; ask someone else.

SOCRATES. It seems that we have here a man who cannot bear being improved and submitting in his own person to the correction that we are talking about.

CALLICLES. I don't feel the smallest interest in anything you say. My only motive in answering you was to oblige Gorgias.

SOCRATES. What are we to do then? Leave the argument in the air?

CALLICLES. You must decide that for yourself.

SOCRATES. One ought not to leave even a story half-told, they say. It should be brought to a point and not left to go about pointless. So answer the rest of my questions, and let our discussion have a fitting end.

CALLICLES. What a bully you are, Socrates. If you take my advice you will let this discussion be, or argue with someone else.

SOCRATES. Who else would be willing? Don't let us leave the matter in this inconclusive state.

CALLICLES. Couldn't you finish the argument alone, either in a continuous speech or answering your questions yourself?

SOCRATES. 'One man doing the work of two' to quote Epicharmus? It looks as if it will have to be like that. But if we are to adopt this method, it must be on condition that we all regard ourselves as rivals in the attempt to distinguish truth from falsehood; we are all equally concerned in the truth being made clear. I will tell you my conclusions; but if any of you think that I am allowing myself to assume what is not true, he must interrupt and challenge me. I am not speaking dogmatically from the certainty of assured knowledge; I am simply your fellow-explorer in the search for truth, and if somebody who contradicts me is obviously right I shall be the first to give way. This is all supposing that you decide that the argument should be continued to its end; otherwise let us give it up and disperse.

GORGIAS. I don't think that we ought to disperse, Socrates, until you have finished the argument, and I am sure that the others agree with me. Personally, I very much want to hear what more you have to say.

SOCRATES. For my part, Gorgias, I should have liked to continue the discussion with Callicles, until I had paid him back an Amphion for his Zethus.[1] However, since you won't collaborate any further, at least listen and interrupt me if you think that I am wrong. If you prove your point I shall not be annoyed with you as you were with me; on the contrary I shall enter your name at the head of my list of benefactors.

CALLICLES. Go on, my good sir, and finish on your own.

SOCRATES. Listen then, while I recapitulate the argument from the start. Is pleasure identical with good? Callicles and I agreed that it is not. – Is pleasure to be sought as a means to good or good as a means to pleasure? Pleasure as a means to good. – Is pleasure something whose presence makes us pleased, and good something whose presence makes us good? Certainly. – But we, and everything else that can be called good, are good by reason of the presence of some excellent quality, are we not? That

1. Cf. p. 80 above and note.

seems an inevitable conclusion, Callicles. – Now the excellence of anything, whether it be an implement or a physical body or a soul or any living being, is not manifested at random in its highest form, but springs from a certain order and rightness and art appropriate in each case. Is that true? In my opinion, yes. – Then the excellence of a thing depends on its having a certain ordered beauty which is the result of arrangement? That is what I should say. – Consequently the presence of the order proper to it is what makes each thing good? So I believe. – It follows that the soul which possesses the appropriate kind of order is better than the disorderly? Obviously. – And a soul which possesses order is orderly? Of course. – And if orderly, disciplined by good sense? Unquestionably. – So the disciplined soul is good after all. I can't see any other conclusion, my dear Callicles, can you? Tell me if you can.

507

CALLICLES. Go on, my good sir.

SOCRATES. I maintain that if a disciplined soul is good, a soul in the opposite condition, which, as we have seen, is a soul marked by folly and licence, will be bad. Certainly. – The man who is disciplined will behave with propriety towards God and man; if he behaved improperly he would not deserve the name of disciplined. That is undeniable. – Again, proper behaviour toward men is uprightness and proper behaviour toward God reverence; and a man who acts uprightly and reverently must be upright and reverent. Certainly. – And not only upright and reverent but brave as well; a disciplined man will not choose inappropriate objects either to pursue or to shun; on the contrary he will pursue or shun the things and people and pleasures and pains that deserve either course, and he will stand his ground firmly where duty requires it. It inevitably follows,

Callicles, that the disciplined man whom we have described, being upright and brave and reverent, will be perfectly good; and a good man does well in all his actions, and because he does well is enviable and happy, whereas the wicked man who does wrong is wretched. Such a person will be the opposite of the undisciplined man, in fact the licentious man, who was the object of your encomium.

That then is the position that I adopt and maintain to be true. If I am right, then it appears that each of us who wants to be happy must pursue and practise self-discipline, and run as fast as his legs will carry him from licentiousness. He must make it his main endeavour not to need correction, but if either he or anyone in whom he is interested, be they individuals or a whole state, should stand in need of it, correction must be inflicted and the penalty paid if happiness is to be achieved.

This seems to me the goal that one should have in view throughout one's life; we can win happiness only by bending all our own efforts and those of the state to the realization of uprightness and self-discipline, not by allowing our appetites to go unchecked, and, in an attempt to satisfy their endless importunity, leading the life of a brigand.

The man who adopts the latter course will win the love neither of God nor of his fellow-men; he is incapable of social life, and without social life there can be no love. We are told on good authority,[1] Callicles, that heaven and earth and their respective inhabitants are held together by the bonds of

508

1. The authority is Pythagorean. According to tradition Pythagoras first gave the name of *Cosmos* to the universe, 'Geometric' or proportional equality, which gives each man his deserts, is spoken of in the *Laws* as the foundation of justice, and is to be enforced by the legislator in preference to simple or 'arithmetic' equality.

society and love and order and discipline and righteousness, and that is why the universe is called an ordered whole or cosmos and not a state of disorder and licence. You, I think, for all your cleverness, have failed to grasp the truth; you have not observed how great a part geometric equality plays in heaven and earth, and because you neglect the study of geometry you preach the doctrine of unfair shares.

However that may be, the choice before you now is either to prove me wrong in my conviction that the happy owe their happiness to the possession of uprightness and discipline and the miserable their misery to the possession of vice, or else, if what I say is true, to examine what follows from it. What follows, Callicles, are all those principles which you questioned my seriousness in enunciating when I said that in the event of any wrong-doing a man should be ready to accuse himself or his son or his friend, and that this was the end for which oratory should be employed. It turns out after all that what you thought Polus admitted out of shame is true, and that doing wrong is not only more disgraceful than suffering wrong but also, in exactly the same degree, more harmful to the doer; and the man who is to be an orator in the proper sense must be upright and understand right and wrong, which is what Polus in his turn accused Gorgias of being ashamed not to admit.

In the light of all this let us consider whether you are right or not, when you reproach me with being unable to defend myself or any of my friends and relations or to save myself from mortal danger, and assert that like an outlaw I am at the mercy of any-one who chooses, if I may adopt your own forcible expression, to slap me on the face, or deprive me of my property, or banish me from my country, or even, in the last resort, put me to death. To be in such a position is the lowest depth of disgrace, according to you; what my opinion is I have already stated several times, but it will bear repetition yet once more.

I maintain, Callicles, that it is not being slapped on the face undeservedly, nor yet being wounded in my body or my purse that is the ultimate disgrace, and that it is more harmful as well as more disgraceful to strike and wound me and mine wrongfully; and that to rob me or enslave me or break into my house, or, generally speaking, to inflict any wrong upon me and mine brings more harm and disgrace upon the wrong-doer than upon me who suffer the wrong.

509

These conclusions, the soundness of which has been already demonstrated in our previous discussion, are, to use a somewhat bold metaphor, held firm and bound fast by a chain of argument as strong as iron or adamant, as far at any rate as I can judge at present; and unless you or someone more radical than you can undo this chain, no one who speaks differently from what I am saying can be right. For my part I follow my invariable principle; I do not claim to know that this is the truth, but I have never met anybody, present company included, who has produced a different opinion without making himself ridiculous.

I assume therefore that this is the truth, and if I am right and wrong-doing is the worst harm that can befall a wrong-doer (though not to be punished for wrong-doing is even worse, if anything can be worse than the worst), what kind of protection will it really be ridiculous for a man not to be able to provide for himself? Surely protection against what does us the greatest harm. There can be no doubt whatever that it is inability to provide this protection for oneself and one's friends and relations which brings the greatest shame; second to this, and after second third, comes helplessness in the face of evil of the second and third degrees of importance, and so on. The glory of being able to protect oneself and the shame of the reverse are directly proportionate to the magnitude of the evil in question. Don't you agree, Callicles?

CALLICLES. Yes.

SOCRATES. Then of these two evils, doing wrong and suffering wrong, the former, we say, is the greater and the latter the less. Now what equipment does a man need to ensure himself protection against both these evils, doing wrong and suffering wrong alike? Is it power or will that is required? What I mean is this; will a man gain exemption from suffering wrong simply by willing not to suffer it, or must he obtain power in order to avert it?

CALLICLES. He must obtain power, obviously.

SOCRATES. But what about doing wrong? Is it sufficient assurance against wrong-doing not to will to do wrong, or must a man in this case too equip himself with some sort of power or skill, at the risk of being involved in wrong-doing if he fails to learn and practise it? Please tell me explicitly, Callicles, whether in your opinion Polus and I were right or not when we found ourselves constrained to agree in our previous discussion that no one does wrong willingly and that all wrong-doing is involuntary.

510 CALLICLES. Take the point for granted, Socrates, if it will hasten the end of the discussion.

SOCRATES. Then it seems that if we are to avoid doing wrong we must acquire some sort of power or skill?

CALLICLES. Yes.

SOCRATES. What then is the skill which will protect us from suffering wrong or reduce that suffering to a minimum? Do you agree with me that it consists in holding office or even absolute power oneself, or else in being a friend of the existing sovereign?

CALLICLES. Absolutely right, Socrates. See how ready I am to applaud you when you talk sense.

SOCRATES. Well, is it also sense to think that the closest friendship is that which exists between men whom the old saw calls 'birds of a feather'? Do you agree?

CALLICLES. Yes.

SOCRATES. So where power is in the hands of a savage and uneducated despot, anyone who is greatly his superior will be an object of fear to the ruler, and never able to be on terms of genuine friendship with him.

CALLICLES. That is true.

SOCRATES. And the same applies to anyone greatly his inferior. In that case the despot will despise him, and never regard him with the esteem due to a friend.

CALLICLES. That is equally true.

SOCRATES. Then the only man left for the despot to make a real friend of is the man of similar character to himself, who shares the same standards and is willing to obey him and submit to his authority. He is the man who will have great power under an absolute government; it is he that no one will injure with impunity, is it not?

CALLICLES. Yes.

SOCRATES. So if a young man under such a government were to ask himself: 'How can I get great power and make myself immune from injury?', the way would seem to lie in accustoming himself from an early age to share the likes and dislikes of his master, and in modelling himself upon him as closely as possible. Agreed?

CALLICLES. Yes.

SOCRATES. Such a man will have achieved the goal of immunity from injury and of possession of great power, as you and your friends would say.

CALLICLES. Certainly.

SOCRATES. But will he have secured himself also against the danger of inflicting wrong? Quite the contrary. Since the master on whom he models himself and whose favour he enjoys is himself a wrong-doer, his own efforts, I suppose, will be directed to being able to inflict the greatest injuries without being punished. Isn't that so?

CALLICLES. Apparently.

SOCRATES. In that case there will befall him the greatest of all evils, a soul vitiated and corrupted by the imitation of his master and the power thus acquired.

CALLICLES. Somehow or other, Socrates, you always contrive to turn things upside down. Don't you know that the imitator we are speaking of will kill your non-imitator, if he chooses, and take away his property?

511 SOCRATES. I should have to be deaf not to know it, my good Callicles, seeing how often I have heard it, from you and from Polus several times before you, and from practically everyone else in Athens. But let me tell you, on the other hand, that your man may kill, if he chooses, but he will be a villain and his victim an honourable man.

CALLICLES. Isn't that exactly what is so revolting?

SOCRATES. Not to a man of sense, as can easily be proved. Do you think that a man ought to make it his chief ambition to prolong his life to the utmost limit, and spend it in the practice of the arts which preserve us from danger, oratory, for example, which you advise me to cultivate as a protection in the law courts?

CALLICLES. And very sound advice it is too.

SOCRATES. Well, my good sir, do you also regard ability to swim as an important accomplishment?

CALLICLES. Good heavens no.

SOCRATES. Yet swimming saves men from death, when they get into a situation that requires it. But if swimming seems to you a triviality, take a more important branch of knowledge, navigation, which, like oratory, saves not only people's lives but also the persons and property which belong to them. Navigation is a modest art that knows her place; she does not put on airs or make out that she has performed some brilliant feat, even though she achieves as much as forensic oratory; she brings a man safe from Aegina for no more than two obols, I believe, and even if he comes from Egypt or Pontus or ever so far away the utmost she charges for this great service, for conveying in safety, as I said, a man and his children and property and womenfolk, is two drachmae when he disembarks at the Piraeus; and the man who possesses this skill and has accomplished all this lands and walks about on the shore beside his ship in a quite unassuming way.

The reason is, I imagine, that he is sensible enough to see that it is quite uncertain which of his passengers he has done a service to by not allowing them to be drowned and which the reverse; he knows that he has landed them in no better condition, physically or spiritually, than when they embarked. So he reflects that, if he has done no good to a man suffering from serious and incurable physical ailments, who is simply to be pitied because he has not gone to the bottom, still less can life be held to be a boon to a man who has a mass of incurable diseases in his soul, which is so much the more precious part of him; it is doing no service to such a man to save him from the sea or the dock or

512

any other danger, the truth being, as the skipper knows, that there is no advantage to the wicked man in continuing to live, seeing that he cannot live other than badly.

That is why the skipper, although he saves our lives, is not in the habit of magnifying his office; and the same may be said, my good sir, of the engineer, whose ability to save is as great as that of a general or any other class of person, let alone a skipper; for an engineer sometimes saves whole cities.[1] You wouldn't think of putting him on the same level as the advocate, would you? Yet if he chose to use big words about his function, like you and your friends, Callicles, he could make out a strong case and overwhelm you with reasons why everybody ought to be an engineer and no other profession is of the smallest importance. All the same you despise him and his art and use the term 'mechanic' as a term of contempt, and you would not hear of marrying your daughter to his son or taking his daughter to wife yourself.

Yet, to go simply by the argument which you advance in praise of your own way of life, what right have you to despise the engineer and the others I have mentioned? You will say, I know, that you are a better man and better born. But if 'better' has a different meaning from the meaning I give it, and the height of excellence consists in keeping oneself and one's property safe, regardless of one's character, it is simply absurd for you to cast aspersions on engineering and medicine and the other professions which exist in order to ensure men's safety. But I beg you, my friend, to conceive it possible that

1. The reference is to the constructors of military engines for the defence as well as the assault of besieged cities. Callicles, of course, shares the habitual contempt of the Athenians for manual workers.

nobility and goodness may be something different from keeping oneself and one's friends from danger, and to consider whether a true man, instead of clinging to life at all costs, ought not to dismiss from his mind the question how long he may have to live. Let him leave that to the will of God in the belief that the womenfolk are right when they tell us that no man can escape his destiny, and let him devote himself to the next problem, how he can best live the life which is allotted to him, and whether he will achieve this by adapting himself to the constitution of the state in which he happens to live. In that case it will be your duty at the present time to model your character as closely as possible on the character of the Athenian people, if you are to gain its affection and acquire great power in the state. Ask yourself whether such a course is really to the advantage of either of us, and take care, my good sir, that we do not suffer the reputed fate of the witches of Thessaly who draw the moon down from the sky; that we do not find, I mean, that we have purchased political power at the cost of all that we hold most dear.[1]

If you believe, Callicles, that anyone can put you in the way of gaining political power in this state and yet remaining, whether for better or worse, unlike it in character, you are in my opinion quite mistaken. It is not a matter of imitation; there must be a genuine natural likeness if you are to make any real progress in the affections of the Athenian Demos, or, for that matter, of Pyrilampes' Demos either. Whoever can make you most like them is the

513

1. Thessaly was famous for witches. The belief that witchcraft injures its practitioners was expressed in a proverbial phrase, 'you are bringing down the moon on yourself', applied to those who bring trouble on themselves. Drawing down the moon was believed to involve loss of the use of sight and limbs.

man who can help you to realize your political and oratorical ambitions; the one Demos, no less than the other, takes pleasure in hearing sentiments which are in harmony with its own nature and detests the reverse. I speak subject to your correction, dear heart, but is there in fact anything to be said against this conclusion, Callicles?

CALLICLES. Somehow or other I can't help being impressed by what you say, Socrates; yet, like most other people, I am not completely convinced.

SOCRATES. That is because the love of Demos in your soul, Callicles, is putting up a resistance to my argument, but perhaps if we go over the same ground more thoroughly you will be convinced. Remember anyhow that we said that body and soul can each of them be treated in two different ways; one way is to gratify their desire for pleasure, and the other is to substitute opposition for gratification with a view to securing their best interests. Isn't that the distinction which we drew at an earlier stage?

CALLICLES. Certainly.

SOCRATES. And the former method, whose aim is pleasure, is dishonourable and simply a form of pandering, is it not?

CALLICLES. Call it so if you like.

SOCRATES. Whereas the latter aims at producing the greatest degree of good in body or soul, whichever is the object of our treatment?

CALLICLES. Certainly.

SOCRATES. Ought we not then to set about our treatment of the state and its citizens on this principle, with the idea of making the citizens themselves as good as possible? Without such a principle, as we discovered earlier, one can do no good; no other service to the state is of the slightest avail if those who are to acquire riches or authority over people

or any other kind of power are not men of good will.   514
May we take that for granted?

CALLICLES. By all means, if you like.

SOCRATES. Suppose, now, Callicles, that with the
idea of embarking upon public life we were advising
one another to undertake a building contract for the
most important type of public works, walls or dockyards or temples. Would it or would it not be our
duty first of all to ask ourselves carefully whether
or not we understood the art of architecture and
from whom we had learnt it?

CALLICLES. It would be our duty of course.

SOCRATES. And a second question would be whether
we had ever put up any private building either for
a friend or for ourselves, and, if so, whether that
building were beautiful or ugly. If it appeared on
investigation that we had had good and reputable
masters and had put up many fine buildings, both
in collaboration with them and on our own after we
ceased to be their pupils, it would be sensible in
those circumstances to venture upon public works.
But if, on the other hand, we could give the name
of no master and point to no buildings standing to
our credit, or only to buildings devoid of all merit,
it would surely be senseless to set our hand to public
works and to urge one another to do so. Is that
right or not?

CALLICLES. Quite right.

SOCRATES. It is the same with everything. Suppose,
for example, that in the belief that we were com-
petent doctors we were urging one another to stand
for a public medical appointment. Presumably we
should submit ourselves to mutual examination on
something like these lines. 'Tell me, pray, what is
Socrates' own state of physical health? Has anybody,
whether slave or free, ever been cured of a disease
by Socrates' treatment?' I should ask the same sort

of questions about you, and if we found that nobody, foreigner or native, slave or free, man or woman, had ever got better through our treatment, we should make ourselves really ridiculous if we were such fools as to attempt to obtain public office ourselves and to advise people like us to do the same, before we had first served a long apprenticeship of trial and error, followed by considerable successful experience of our profession in private practice. We should be like the man in the proverb who began his apprenticeship as a potter by trying his hand at a wine-jar. Don't you think that such behaviour would be senseless?

CALLICLES. Yes.

515 SOCRATES. Now let us take our own position, my good sir. You have lately embarked on a public career and are urging me to do the same and reproaching me for my reluctance. Surely then this is the moment for mutual examination. Has any citizen hitherto become a better man through the influence of Callicles? Is there anyone, foreign or native, slave or free, who owes to Callicles his conversion to virtue from a previous wicked career of wrong-doing and debauchery and folly? What will you say if you are asked this question, Callicles? What example will you give of a man who has been improved by associating with you? Why hesitate to answer, if you can point to any achievement of yours in this line while you were still a private person before you entered politics?

CALLICLES. You're always set upon victory, Socrates.

SOCRATES. Not in the least; my question is inspired by a genuine wish to know your ideas on the proper conduct of political life at Athens. Surely your sole concern as a public man will be to make us who are citizens as good as possible. Have we not already agreed more than once that that is the duty of the statesman? Pray let us have an answer; yes or no. Well, I will answer for you; we *have* agreed. Then if this is the service which a good man owes to his country, turn your mind once more to the people you mentioned a while ago, Pericles and Cimon and Miltiades and Themistocles, and tell me whether you still think that they were good citizens.

CALLICLES. I do.

SOCRATES. In that case each of them must clearly have left the citizens better than he found them. Did he do so or not?

CALLICLES. Yes, he did.

SOCRATES. Then when Pericles first appeared on a public platform the citizens were in a worse state than when he made his last speeches.

CALLICLES. Perhaps.

SOCRATES. It isn't a question of perhaps, my friend; it is a necessary consequence of what we have agreed, if he really was a good citizen.

CALLICLES. What of it, then?

SOCRATES. Nothing; just tell me this; are the Athenians supposed to have been improved by Pericles' influence or on the contrary to have been corrupted by him? The latter is what I am told; people say that Pericles made the Athenians lazy and cowardly and garrulous and covetous by his introduction of the system of payment for services to the state.

CALLICLES. The people who tell you that are pro-Spartans with cauliflower ears, Socrates.[1]

SOCRATES. There is one thing, however, that I know positively from my own experience, not from hearsay, and so do you. At the beginning of his career Pericles' reputation was high, and no sentence involving disgrace was ever passed on him by the

1. It was regarded as a sign of pro-Spartan sympathies to be addicted to boxing.

Athenians, who were *ex hypothesi* worse at that time than they subsequently became; but when he had converted them to honourable courses, at the end of his life, they convicted him of embezzlement and came near to condemning him to death, obviously because they believed him to be a villain.

CALLICLES. What of that? Does that make Pericles a bad man?

SOCRATES. Well, we should have a poor opinion of a man in charge of asses or horses or oxen, who found the beasts free from any tendency to kick or butt or bite, and handed them over at the end of his time in a ferocious state with all these vices developed. Don't you think that any man is a bad keeper of any animal, whatever it may be, who leaves it fiercer than he found it? Yes or no?

CALLICLES. Yes, if it will give you pleasure to hear me say so.

SOCRATES. Give me the additional pleasure of an answer to this question too. Is man one of the animals or not?

CALLICLES. Of course he is.

SOCRATES. And Pericles was in charge of men?

CALLICLES. Yes.

SOCRATES. Well then; if Pericles was a good statesman, ought not his charges to have become more virtuous and less vicious under his influence? That is what we agreed just now.

CALLICLES. Certainly.

SOCRATES. And according to Homer the virtuous are gentle. Do you concur in that opinion?

CALLICLES. Yes.

SOCRATES. Yet Pericles made his charges fiercer than he found them, and what is more, fiercer towards himself, which is the last thing he would have wished.

CALLICLES. Do you want me to agree?

SOCRATES. If what I am saying seems true.

CALLICLES. Very well, let it be so.

SOCRATES. Now, if they were fiercer, they were more vicious and less good.

CALLICLES. Granted.

SOCRATES. Then by this reasoning Pericles was not a good statesman.[1]

CALLICLES. That is what *you* say.

SOCRATES. Not at all; you are involved as well by your own admissions. But tell me now about Cimon. Did not the people whose minister he was ostracize him in order that they might not hear his voice for ten years?[2] And they did the same to Themistocles,

1. The intemperance of this criticism of Pericles is explicable only by the bitterness of Plato's feelings about politics in general. Pericles was notable for the moral authority which enabled him to withstand popular feeling and to persuade the Athenians to embrace unpleasant courses; an example is the policy adopted in 431 B.C. of abandoning Attica to the Spartans and concentrating the population within the city.

The charge of debauching the Athenians by the introduction of pay for public services refers principally to the introduction of pay for service on juries. This was sufficient for a bare livelihood, and the unfortunate effect on the poorer citizens is the object of Aristophanes' satire in the *Wasps*.

Pericles maintained his ascendancy for thirty years, and it was only the plague of 430 B.C. that turned the Athenians against him. He was found guilty of the misappropriation of a sum so trifling that the verdict amounted to an acquittal, and, though he was fined, he was shortly afterwards re-elected as general. He died in the following year. The version of this episode given in the text is little less than a travesty of the facts.

2. Ostracism involved absence from Athens for ten years, but without any loss of rights or property. Cimon, the son of Miltiades, prosecuted the war against Persia in the years following the Persian invasion, and won a great victory at the river Eurymedon in 468 B.C. He was an oligarch in politics whose policy was to retain the friendship of Sparta, and when this policy broke down in 462 he was ostracized. He was, however, recalled to make a truce with Sparta in 457, and died in 450 in command of an expedition sent to prevent the re-establishment of Persian power in Cyprus.

and punished him with exile besides.[1] As for Miltiades of Marathon, they condemned him to be thrown into the pit appointed for criminals, and, but for the President of the Council, that is what would have happened to him.[2] Yet if these people had been good men, as you assert, they would never have met such fates. You never find a good charioteer who begins by keeping his balance, and later, when he has trained his team and increased his own expertise, comes to grief. That simply does not happen, either in driving or in any other activity. Do you think it does?

CALLICLES. No.

SOCRATES. It seems then that what we said before is true, that we know of no one who has been a good statesman in this country. You admitted that there is none now living, but declared that there had been such in the past and selected these four men. But now it appears that they were no better than the men of our time, and if they were orators the oratory that they employed was neither the genuine kind – in that case they would not have fallen from power – nor the kind which we have called pandering.[3]

1. Themistocles, the saviour of Greece at Salamis and the creator of Athenian naval power, was ostracized *c.* 472 B.C. for reasons which are obscure. Later he was accused of holding treasonable communications with Persia, and fled to Asia Minor to avoid arrest and trial. It is unlikely that he was guilty, but the charge led to his finally placing his services at the disposal of the Persian king, who rewarded him with the government of Magnesia, where he died.

2. Miltiades, the hero of Marathon in 490 B.C., was condemned after an abortive attack on Paros for 'deceiving the people' by employing their forces in a private quarrel. He was heavily fined, and, according to Herodotus, escaped a capital sentence on the ground of his former services. The 'pit' was a place into which the bodies of executed criminals were thrown, though some late commentators believed that men were thrown into it alive.

3. The statesmen in question failed either to make men better,

CALLICLES. But yet, Socrates, none of the men of today comes anywhere near equalling the achievements of any of the four men in question.

SOCRATES. My dear sir, I find no more fault with them than you do as servants of the state; indeed they seem to me to have been better servants than the present people, and more able to provide the state with what it desired. But when it is a matter of diverting men's desires into a new channel instead of allowing them free course, or of driving one's fellows by persuasion or constraint to the adoption of measures designed for their improvement, which is the sole duty of a good citizen, there is practically nothing to choose between your men and their successors, though I grant you that the men of old showed much more cleverness than our contemporaries in the provision of ships and walls and dockyards and the like.

Discussion between you and me is an absurd affair; all the time we have been talking we have never ceased to revolve in an endless circle of mutual misunderstanding. All the same I believe that on several occasions you have admitted and realized that dealing with men's bodies and souls is a twofold business. One way of proceeding is to behave as their servant; that is how the body is provided with food when it is hungry, drink when it is thirsty, clothes, blankets, and shoes when it is cold, and has all its other desires satisfied as they arise; I am purposely using the same illustrations in order to make the matter clearer to you. The purveyor of these wants may be a shopkeeper or a

---

which is the object of the true oratory, or to gratify their inclinations, which is the object of the false. In view of Socrates' next speech it is odd that they should be said not to have succeeded in false oratory; presumably what is meant is that if they had *thoroughly* gratified the public they would not have incurred its hostility.

wholesale merchant or the actual producer of one
of the articles in question, a baker or cook or weaver
or shoemaker or tanner; it is no wonder if such
people become possessed with the idea that they are
the real authors of the body's welfare and inspire
the same belief in others, in everyone in fact who
does not know that beside all these occupations
there exist the arts of the trainer and the doctor, and
that these constitute genuine physical culture; it is
their province to control all these other crafts and
make use of their products, because they alone know
what kinds of food and drink have a tendency to
promote physical excellence or the reverse. This is
a subject of which the other crafts are entirely
ignorant, and that is why among the occupations
that deal with the body they should be classed as
servile and menial and unworthy of a free man,
whereas the arts of training and medicine have every
right to be called their masters.

518

When I tell you that the same situation exists with
regard to the soul, you sometimes seem to understand and express agreement as if you knew what
I meant, but a moment later you come out with an
assertion that excellent men are to be found among
the citizens of this state, and when I ask you who
they are the names of the politicians you bring forward are such as to make me think that, if my
question were about physical training and I asked
you to give the names of good authorities past or
present on physical culture, you would answer quite
seriously that Thearion the baker and Mithaecus
the author of the Sicilian cookery book and Saram-
bus the retail dealer are wonderful authorities on
physical culture, because of the wonderful cakes,
food, and wine that they respectively provide.

Probably you would be vexed with me if I were
to say to you: 'My man, you know nothing at all

about physical training. The people you mention are mere servants and caterers to the desires, devoid of any sound or true knowledge of their nature; they are the sort of people who may well win men's praise by cramming and fattening their bodies, and afterwards cause them to lose even the flesh they had; and the victims in their ignorance, instead of holding the purveyors of their feasts responsible for their ailments and loss of weight, will throw the blame on whoever happen to be their associates and advisers at a considerably later date, when their surfeit in defiance of the laws of health brings sickness in its train. They will reinforce the reproaches which they cast on their advisers by positive injuries, if they have the power to inflict them, while they continue aloud in the praises of those who are the real authors of their troubles.'

You now, Callicles, are behaving in just the same way as these gluttons; you are extolling men who have regaled the Athenians by giving them their fill of what they desired, and people say that they have made Athens great; what they do not perceive is that through the efforts of these earlier statesmen it is bloated and rotten to the core. They have glutted the state with harbours and dockyards and walls and tribute and rubbish of that sort, regardless of the requirements of moderation and righteousness, and when the inevitable fit of weakness supervenes the citizens will hold their current advisers responsible, and go on extolling Themistocles and Cimon and Pericles, the real authors of their woes. Possibly, when they begin to lose their old possessions as well as their recent acquisitions, they will, if you are not careful, even attack you and my friend Alcibiades,[1] who may perhaps be responsible in a minor degree for the crisis, though you were not its originators.

519

1. Cf. note, p. 75.

There is one piece of folly which I see being practised today besides hearing it reported from earlier times. When the state attempts to bring any of its public men to account as wrong-doers, I find that they take it very hard and raise a great outcry that they are being monstrously treated; their complaint is that after all the benefits they have conferred on the state it is most unfair that they should come to ruin at its hands. Now all that is pure moonshine. No head of state could ever have ruin inflicted on him by the very state over which he presides unless he deserved it. The same seems to be true of those who profess to be statesmen as of those who profess to be teachers of goodness. These latter, for all their wisdom, are apt to fall into a strange inconsistency; professing to be teachers of goodness they often accuse their pupils of wronging them by cheating them of their fees and in other ways not making a proper return for the benefits they have received. What can be more illogical than to suppose that men who have become good and upright by losing their tendency to wrong-doing and by acquiring righteousness through the teaching of their master should commit wrong by the exercise of a quality that they no longer possess? Don't you think that strange, my friend? By your refusal to answer you have compelled me to hold forth like a regular stump orator, Callicles.

CALLICLES. But surely you can speak without having to have someone to answer you.

SOCRATES. Apparently I can; on this occasion anyhow, for lack of an answer from you, I am making my harangue interminably prolix. But tell me for friendship's sake, don't you think it absurd for a man who claims to have made somebody virtuous to find fault with his convert for being a scoundrel, when he has become virtuous under his instruction and still remains so?

CALLICLES. I certainly do.

SOCRATES. And don't you frequently hear those who profess to instruct mankind in virtue making this sort of complaint?

CALLICLES. Yes, I do; but why waste words on such worthless creatures?   520

SOCRATES. Then what are we to say of men who profess to guide the state and to make its perfection their chief concern, but yet are quite ready to accuse it of supreme wickedness when occasion arises? Are they any better than the people I have mentioned? The fact is, my good sir, as I was saying to Polus, that there is practically nothing to choose between the popular teacher and the orator; it is merely ignorance that makes you regard the latter as beyond praise and despise the former.[1] In actual truth the art of the teacher ranks as far above oratory as legislation above the administration of justice or physical culture above medicine. But it has always appeared to me that teachers and orators are the only people to whom it is not open to blame the object of their instruction for behaving badly towards themselves, unless they are prepared in the same breath to accuse themselves of not having done the good that they profess to have done. Isn't that so?

CALLICLES. Undoubtedly.

SOCRATES. And they are also the only people who could reasonably be expected to give their services free without payment if what they profess is true.

1. Callicles, though he treats a man as distinguished as Gorgias with respect, despises sophists in general; compare his behaviour towards Polus. The orator whom he admires is not the teacher of oratory but the politician who successfully practises it. To Plato both sophists and politicians are 'panders', and, though distinguishable, near akin; cf. with this passage p. 47 above.

In any other case, as when, for instance, a man improves his pace as a runner through the services of a trainer, there is a possibility that the pupil might cheat the expert of his due if the latter gave his services free, without making a definite bargain in advance and receiving payment as nearly as possible at the time he imparts the secret of speed. I suppose you would agree that it is not slowness of foot but a tendency to wrong-doing that causes a man to inflict a wrong?

CALLICLES. Yes.

SOCRATES. So a man who removes a tendency to wrong-doing is in no danger of being wronged; he is the only person who could safely give his services free, provided that he really possessed the ability to make people good. Agreed?

CALLICLES. Certainly.

SOCRATES. Presumably that is why there is no discredit in a man receiving payment for his advice on any other subject, architecture, for instance, or some similar art?

CALLICLES. Presumably.

SOCRATES. But when one is dealing with the question how a man can perfect his character and best manage either his own household or the state, it is reckoned discreditable, isn't it, to refuse to give one's advice except for payment?

CALLICLES. Yes.

SOCRATES. Obviously the reason is that this is the only service which makes the recipient eager to make a return in kind; so if the performer of the service gets back the same treatment as he gave, it is good evidence that his efforts have been successful, and *vice versa*. Is that so?

521 CALLICLES. It is.

SOCRATES. Tell me then which kind of approach you would have me adopt towards the state. Am I to withstand the Athenians with the idea of improving them, like a doctor, or to behave like a servant whose object is simply to do his master's pleasure? Tell me the truth, Callicles; you began by speaking your mind frankly, and I have a right to expect you to continue in the same way; out with it now like a man.

CALLICLES. What I say then is that you should be the state's servant.

SOCRATES. So in fact you are urging me, my noble fellow, to be a pander.

CALLICLES. Yes, if you prefer to use the vilest name for it.[1] Otherwise –

SOCRATES. Don't tell me once more that my life will be at the mercy of anyone who pleases, or I shall repeat that in that case I shall be the innocent victim of a villain; nor yet that I shall be stripped of my possessions, or I shall tell you again that the man who strips me will gain nothing from his spoil. Having acquired it by wrong he will make a wrong use of it, and wrong involves shame, and shame harm to himself.

CALLICLES. You seem to me, Socrates, as confident that none of these things will happen to you as if you were living in another world and were not liable to be dragged into court, possibly by some scoundrel of the vilest character.

SOCRATES. I should be a fool, Callicles, if I didn't realize that in this state anything may happen to anybody. But this at least I am sure of, that, if I am brought to trial on a charge involving any of the penalties you mention, my prosecutor will be a villain, for no honest man would prosecute an innocent party. And it would not be at all surprising

1. Literally 'if you prefer the name of Mysian'. The people of Mysia were regarded as the vilest of mankind, and various proverbial expressions were founded on the name of 'Mysian'.

if I were executed. Would you like to know why I
expect this?

CALLICLES. Very much.

SOCRATES. I believe that I am one of the few
Athenians – perhaps indeed there is no other – who
studies the genuine art of statemanship, and that I
am the only man now living who puts it into practice. So because what I say on any occasion is not
designed to please, and because I aim not at what is
most agreeable but at what is best, and will not
employ the subtle arts which you advise, I shall have
no defence to offer in a court of law. I can only
repeat what I was saying to Polus; I shall be like a
doctor brought before a tribunal of children at the
suit of a confectioner. Imagine what sort of defence
a man like that could make before such a court if he
were accused in the following terms: 'Children, the
accused has committed a number of crimes against
you; he is the ruin of even the youngest among you
with his surgery and cautery; he reduces you to a
522   state of helpless misery by choking you with bitter
draughts and inflicting upon you a regime of star-
vation which cuts you off from food and drink.
What a contrast to the abundant and varied luxury
with which I have entertained you.' What do you
think that the doctor could find to say in such a
plight? If he were to utter the truth and tell the
children that he had done all these things in the
interest of their health, think of the prodigious
outcry that a court so constituted would raise.

CALLICLES. Perhaps it would; one would have to be
prepared for it.

SOCRATES. Then don't you think that the accused
would be at his wit's end for a reply?

CALLICLES. No doubt he would.

SOCRATES. Well, that is the situation in which I am
sure that I shall find myself if I come before a court

of law. I shall not be able to point to any pleasures that I have provided for my judges, the only kind of service and good turn that they recognize; indeed I see nothing to envy either in those who purvey or those who receive such services. And if it is alleged against me either that I am the ruin of the younger people by reducing them to a state of helpless doubt[1] or that I insult their elders by bitter criticism in public or in private no defence will avail me, whether true or not, the truth being simply that in all that I say I am guided by what is right and that my actions are in the interest of those who are sitting in judgement on me. So presumably I shall have no alternative but to submit to my fate, whatever it may be.

CALLICLES. Do you really think, Socrates, that all is well with a man in such a position who cannot defend himself before his country?

SOCRATES. I do think so, Callicles, provided that he has at his disposal the form of self-defence whose strength you have yourself frequently acknowledged, the defence which consists in never having committed an offence against God or man either in word or deed. This, as we have agreed more than once, is the best of all kinds of self-defence. If it were proved against me that I was incapable of procuring for myself or helping others to procure this sort of defence, I should be deeply ashamed, whether the tribunal which convicted me were large or small, or even if it consisted of but a single person. If this incapacity were to be the cause of my death I should feel great distress; but if I were to come to my end for lack of the pander's type of oratory, I am sure that you would see me facing my fate with serenity. The mere act of dying has no terror for anyone not

1. One charge brought against Socrates at his trial was that he had corrupted the young men of Athens.

utterly devoid of sense and manliness; it is wrong-doing that is terrible; for to enter the next world with one's soul loaded with sins is the supreme misfortune. I can tell you a story that proves this, if you like.

CALLICLES. Well, since you have finished with all your other points, you may as well round things off.

523 SOCRATES. Give ear then, as they say, to a very fine story, which will, I suppose, seem fiction to you but is fact to me; what I am going to tell you I tell you as the truth.

Homer relates that, when they succeeded their father, Zeus and Poseidon and Pluto divided his empire between them.[1] Now there was in the time of Cronus a law concerning mankind which has remained in force among the gods from that time to this. The law ordains that, when his time comes to die, a man who has lived a righteous and pure life shall depart to the isles of the blessed and there remain in complete felicity, free from sorrow, but that the man whose life has been wicked and godless shall be imprisoned in the place of retribution and judgement, which is called Tartarus.[2]

In the time of Cronus and in the early days of the reign of Zeus men were tried during their life-time by living judges on the very day on which they were fated to die. This led to perversion of justice, so Pluto and the overseers of the isles of the blessed came to Zeus and complained that men were arriving at both destinations contrary to their deserts. Then Zeus said: 'I will put an end to this. The cause of

1. Homer, *Iliad* xv, ll. 187 *ff.*

2. Hesiod places the heroes of the Trojan War in Isles of the Blessed conceived as actual places on the surface of the earth, and later they become the general abode of the righteous after death. Similarly Tartarus, which in Homer is the prison-house of the Titans, becomes for Plato the place of torture for all wrong-doers.

this miscarriage of justice is that men, being tried in their life-time are tried in their clothes. Many whose souls are wicked are dressed in the trappings of physical beauty and high birth and riches, and when their trial takes place they are supported by a crowd of witnesses, who come to testify to the righteousness of their lives. This causes confusion to the judges, who are also hampered by being clothed themselves, so that their soul's vision is clouded by the physical veil of eyes and ears and the rest of the body, and their own vesture as well as the accused's constitutes an obstacle between them and the truth. Our first task, then,' said Zeus, 'is to take from men the foreknowledge of the hour of their death which they at present enjoy. I have charged Prometheus to bring this to an end.[1] Next, they must all be tried naked, that is, when they are dead, and to ensure complete justice the judge too must be naked and dead himself, viewing with bare soul the bare soul of every man as soon as he is dead, when he has no kinsmen to aid him and has left behind on earth all his former glory. The need of this became apparent to me sooner than to you, and I have appointed three of my own sons as judges, two from Asia, Minos and Rhadamanthus, and one 524 from Europe, Aeacus.[2] These, when they are dead, shall sit in judgement in the meadow at the parting

1. Prometheus, who gives foresight, can also take it away. There may be here an echo of Aeschylus, *Prometheus Vinctus*, ll. 248 ff., where Prometheus explains that he stopped mortals from foreseeing their fate by implanting in them a tendency to hope against hope.

2. The Greeks of Plato's time recognized only two main divisions of the world, Europe and Asia. Minos and Rhadamanthus, sons of Zeus and Europa, were born in Crete, of which Minos became king; Crete therefore is presumably reckoned by Plato as part of Asia. Aeacus, the son of Zeus and Aegina, was born in the island later named after his mother. All these are judges in Hades in quite early tradition.

of the ways from which the two roads lead, the one to the isles of the blessed and the other to Tartarus. Rhadamanthus shall try the men of Asia and Aeacus the men of Europe, but to Minos I will give the supreme function of delivering judgement when his colleagues are in doubt. This will ensure that men's ultimate destiny is decided in accordance with perfect justice.'

This, Callicles, is what I have heard and believe to be true, and from this account I draw the following conclusions. Death, it seems to me, is nothing but the divorce of two separate entities, body and soul, and, when this divorce takes place, each of them is left in much the same state as it reached during the man's life. The body retains its natural characteristics with the consequences of training and accident still visible. For instance, if a man's body during life has grown tall by nature or nurture or both, his corpse will be tall in death; if fat, his corpse will be fat, and so on. Again, if the deceased was in the habit of wearing his hair long, his corpse will be long-haired; if he was a convict, whose body was marked during life with the scars of blows inflicted by the cat or in other ways, the same marks will be apparent after death; if his limbs were broken or deformed in life you will see the same when he is dead. In a word, all or almost all the physical characteristics which a man has acquired during life remain visible for a time even when he is no more. The same, I believe, Callicles, is true of the soul; once it is stripped of the body all its qualities may be seen, not only its natural endowments but the modifications effected in it by the various habits which its owner has formed.

So when the dead reach the judgement-seat, in the case of Asiatics the judgement seat of Rhadamanthus, Rhadamanthus summons them before him and inspects each man's soul, without knowing to whom it belongs. Often, when it is the king of Persia or some other monarch or potentate that he has to deal with, he finds that there is no soundness in the soul whatever; it is a mass of weals and scars 525 imprinted on it by the various acts of perjury and wrong-doing of which the man has been guilty; it is twisted and warped by lies and vanity and quite out of the straight because truth has had no part in its development. Power, luxury, pride, and debauchery have left it so full of disproportion and ugliness that when he has inspected it Rhadamanthus despatches it in ignominy straight to prison, where on its arrival it will undergo the appropriate treatment.

The object of all punishment which is rightly inflicted should be either to improve and benefit its subject or else to make him an example to others, who will be deterred by the sight of his sufferings and reform their own conduct. The men who are helped by undergoing punishment, whether by God or man, are those whose faults are remediable; yet both in this world and the next this benefit is procurable only at the cost of pain and anguish; there is no other way in which men can be cured of wrong-doing. Those who have committed the deadliest sins and are consequently incurable form the class which furnishes examples to others. Being incurable they are no longer capable of receiving benefit themselves, but they do good to others, who see them suffering an eternity of the most severe and painful and terrible torment on account of their sins. They are literally hung up as object-lessons there in the prison-house of Hades, in order that every newly-arrived sinner may contemplate them and take the warning to heart.

If what Polus says about him is true, I have no

hesitation in asserting that Archelaus will be found in this second category, together with any other dictator of like character. Indeed, I think that the majority of these exemplary sufferers are drawn from among dictators and kings and potentates and public men, whose power gives them the opportunity of committing the greatest and most deadly sins. In support of this view I can quote Homer, in whose Hades those whose punishment is everlasting, Tantalus and Sisyphus and Tityos,[1] are kings and potentates, whereas Thersites[2] – and the same holds good of other bad men in a private station – has never been represented as suffering the extremity of torment assigned to the hopelessly damned. The reason is, no doubt, that he had smaller opportunities of wrong-doing, and to that extent was more fortunate than those whose scope was unlimited.

However, Callicles, even if the worst sinners are found among men in power, there is nothing to prevent good men arising in this class, and those who do so are greatly to be admired. The difficulty of living a life of complete righteousness when one has unbounded power to do wrong is such that the man who overcomes it deserves the highest praise. But such men are rare. There have been, both here and in other countries, and no doubt will be hereafter, men who have shone in the righteous conduct of affairs committed to their charge; one of the most illustrious, Aristides the son of Lysimachus, won a reputation which extended over the whole of Greece;[3] but the majority of men in power, my good sir, are bad.

1. The punishment of these three rulers is described in *Odyssey* XI, ll. 576 *ff.*

2. Thersites, a subordinate in the Greek army at Troy, abuses the leaders of the expedition in *Iliad* II, ll. 211 *ff.*, and is chastised by Odysseus.

3. Aristides, whose reputation for uprightness earned him

As I was saying, then, when Rhadamanthus gets such a person before him, he is quite ignorant of his identity or parentage; his knowledge is confined to the man's guilt; and having considered this and made a mark to indicate whether he regards him as curable or incurable, he despatches him to Tartarus, where he undergoes the appropriate treatment. Sometimes the eye of the judge lights on a soul which has lived in purity and truth; it may or may not be the soul of a private person, but most often, Callicles, if I am not mistaken, it is the soul of a lover of wisdom who has kept to his own calling during his life and not been meddlesome; then Rhadamanthus is struck with admiration and dismisses him to the isles of the blessed. Aeacus discharges the same judicial function, holding, like Rhadamanthus, a staff of office in his hand; Minos, who sits as president of the court, enjoys the unique distinction of a golden sceptre; you may remember that Odysseus in Homer says that he saw him 'wielding a sceptre of gold and pronouncing judgement in Hades'.[1]

Personally, Callicles, I put faith in this story, and make it my aim to present my soul to its judge in the soundest possible state. That is why, dismissing from consideration the honours which stimulate most men's ambition, I shall keep my gaze fixed on the truth and aspire to perfection, both in life and,

---

the name of 'the Just', fought at Salamis and commanded the Athenian contingent at Plataea. Subsequently he was one of the chief organizers of the Confederacy of Delos and assessed the contributions of the members. Since he suffered ostracism during his career, the praise for which he is here singled out seems inconsistent with the criticism of Pericles and the rest on the ground of their political misfortunes and with the principle proclaimed above (p. 136) that no statesman ever fell from power without deserving to do so.

1. *Odyssey* XI, l. 569.

when my time comes to die, in death. To this way of life and to this struggle, in which the prize, I assure you, outweighs all the prizes of this world, I challenge all men to the best of my ability. In your case, Callicles, it is a counter-challenge, coupled with the reproach that when the moment comes for you to stand the trial of which I have just spoken you will be quite unable to defend yourself; you will stand at the judgement-seat of the son of Aegina, when he summons you before him, as gaping and dizzy as Socrates before an earthly tribunal; possibly someone will slap you on the face with impunity and subject you to every kind of insult.

527

Perhaps you may despise what I have told you as no more than an old wives' tale. There would be every reason why you should if our search had disclosed to us any better or truer account of the matter; but as things are you see that the three of you, yourself and Polus and Gorgias, the wisest men in Greece, are unable to show that there is any better way of life than this, which has the further advantage of being plainly in our interest in the world to come. All the other theories put forward in our long conversation have been refuted and this conclusion alone stands firm, that one should avoid doing wrong with more care than being wronged, and that the supreme object of a man's efforts, in public and in private life, must be the reality rather than the appearance of goodness. Moreover, if a man goes wrong in any way he must be punished, and the next best thing to being good is to become good by submitting to punishment and paying the penalty for one's faults. Every form of pandering, whether to oneself or to others, whether to large groups or to small, is to be shunned; oratory is to be employed only in the service of right, and the same holds true of every other activity.

Be guided by me then and join me in the pursuit of what, as our argument shows, will secure your happiness both here and hereafter. Let people despise you for a fool and insult you if they will; nay, even if they inflict the last indignity of a blow, take it cheerfully; if you are really a good man devoted to the practice of virtue they can do you no harm.

When we have adequately exercised ourselves in this way in partnership with one another, we can, if we think fit, set our hand to politics or to giving our opinion about any other subject that attracts us: our opinions will be better worth having then than they are now. It would be shameful for men in our present condition, who are so ignorant that we never think the same for two moments together, even on subjects of the greatest importance, to give ourselves the airs of persons of weight. Let us then allow ourselves to be led by the truth now revealed to us, which teaches that the best way of life is to practice righteousness and virtue, whether living or dying; let us follow that way and urge others to follow it, instead of the way which you in mistaken confidence are urging upon me; it is quite worthless, Callicles.

SELECT BIBLIOGRAPHY

Dodds, E. R. *Gorgias* (text and commentary). Oxford University Press, 1959.

Thompson, W. H. *Plato's Gorgias* (text and commentary). Bell & Sons, 4th ed. 1915.

Guthrie, W. K. C. Plato, *Protagoras and Meno*. Penguin Classics, 1956.

Hamilton, W. Plato, *Phaedrus* and *The Seventh and Eighth Letters*. Penguin Classics, 1973.

Lee, H. D. P. Plato, *Republic*. Penguin Classics, 1955.

Burnet, J. *Greek Philosophy, Thales to Plato*. Macmillan, 1914, reprinted 1968.

Cornford, F. M. *Before and After Socrates*. Cambridge University Press, 1932, reprinted 1964.

Field, G. C. *Plato and his Contemporaries*. Methuen, 3rd ed. 1967.

Grube, G. M. A. *Plato's Thought*. Methuen, 1935.

Shorey, P. *What Plato Said*. Chicago, 1933 (abridged ed. 1965).

Taylor, A. E. *Plato, the Man and his Work*. Methuen, 7th ed. reprinted 1966.

INDEX

FOR THE BEST IN PAPERBACKS, LOOK FOR THE

In every corner of the world, on every subject under the sun, Penguin represents quality and variety – the very best in publishing today.

For complete information about books available from Penguin – including Pelicans, Puffins, Peregrines and Penguin Classics – and how to order them, write to us at the appropriate address below. Please note that for copyright reasons the selection of books varies from country to country.

In the United Kingdom: For a complete list of books available from Penguin in the U.K., please write to *Dept E.P., Penguin Books Ltd, Harmondsworth, Middlesex, UB7 0DA*

In the United States: For a complete list of books available from Penguin in the U.S., please write to *Dept BA, Penguin, 299 Murray Hill Parkway, East Rutherford, New Jersey 07073*

In Canada: For a complete list of books available from Penguin in Canada, please write to *Penguin Books Canada Ltd, 2801 John Street, Markham, Ontario L3R 1B4*

In Australia: For a complete list of books available from Penguin in Australia, please write to the *Marketing Department, Penguin Books Australia Ltd, P.O. Box 257, Ringwood, Victoria 3134*

In New Zealand: For a complete list of books available from Penguin in New Zealand, please write to the *Marketing Department, Penguin Books (NZ) Ltd, Private Bag, Takapuna, Auckland 9*

In India: For a complete list of books available from Penguin, please write to *Penguin Overseas Ltd, 706 Eros Apartments, 56 Nehru Place, New Delhi, 110019*

In Holland: For a complete list of books available from Penguin in Holland, please write to *Penguin Books Nederland B.V., Postbus 195, NL–1380 AD Weesp, Netherlands*

In Germany: For a complete list of books available from Penguin, please write to *Penguin Books Ltd, Friedrichstrasse 10 – 12, D–6000 Frankfurt Main 1, Federal Republic of Germany*

In Spain: For a complete list of books available from Penguin in Spain, please write to *Longman Penguin España, Calle San Nicolas 15, E–28013 Madrid, Spain*

PROTAGORAS AND MENO

Translated by W. K. C. Guthrie

Plato held that philosophy must be a product of living contact between mind and mind, and his dialogues afforded him the means of reaching a wide audience. *Protagoras*, possibly his dramatic masterpiece, deals, like *Meno*, with the problem of teaching the art of successful living and good citizenship. While *Protagoras* keeps to the level of practical commonsense, *Meno* leads on into the heart of Plato's philosophy, the immortality of the soul and the doctrine that learning is knowledge acquired before birth.

THE LAST DAYS OF SOCRATES

Translated by Hugh Tredennick

In the four works which compose this volume – *Euthyphro*, *The Apology*, *Crito*, and *Phaedo* – Plato, his most devoted disciple, has preserved for us the essence of Socrates' teaching and the logical system of question and answer he perfected in order to define the nature of virtue and knowledge. The vindication of Socrates and the pathos of his death are admirably conveyed in Hugh Tredennick's modern translation.

THE LAWS

Translated by T. J. Saunders

The reader of *The Republic* may well be astonished by *The Laws*. Instead of an ideal state ruled directly by moral philosophers, this later work depicts a society permeated by the rule of law. Immutable laws control most aspects of public and private life, from civil and legal administration to marriage, religion and sport. The rigours of life in Plato's utopian Republic are not much tempered here, but *The Laws* is a much more practical approach to Plato's ideal.

THE REPUBLIC

Translated by Desmond Lee

The Republic, perhaps the best known of Plato's dialogues, is an attempt to apply the principles of his philosophy to political affairs. Ostensibly a discussion of the nature of Justice, it lays before us Plato's vision of the ideal state, covering a wide range of topics, social, educational, psychological, moral and philosophical. It also includes, in the process, some of Plato's most important writing on the nature of reality and the theory of 'forms'. Plato is critical of Athenian Democracy, which had been responsible for the execution of his friend and teacher, Socrates, and his political ideas, as expressed in The Republic, started lines of thought which are still relevant today.

TIMAEUS AND CRITIAS

Translated by Desmond Lee

The Timaeus, in which Plato attempted a scientific explanation of the universe's origin, is the earliest Greek account of a divine creation: as such it has significantly influenced European thought, even down to the present day. Yet this dialogue and, even more, its unfinished sequel, the Critias, have latterly attracted equal attention as the sources of the Atlantis legend.

THE SYMPOSIUM

Translated by Walter Hamilton

The Symposium – a masterpiece of dramatic dialogue – is set at a dinner party to which are invited several of the literary celebrities of Athenian society. After dinner it is proposed that each member of the company should make a speech in praise of love. A full discussion follows and the dialogue ends with a brilliant character sketch of Socrates by Alcibiades.

Also published

PHAEDRUS and LETTERS VII and VIII

Aeschylus	**The Oresteia**
	(Agamemnon/Choephori/Eumenides)
	Prometheus Bound/The Suppliants/Seven
	Against Thebes/The Persians
Aesop	**Fables**
Apollonius of Rhodes	**The Voyage of Argo**
Apuleius	**The Golden Ass**
Aristophanes	**The Knights/Peace/The Birds/The Assembly**
	Women/Wealth
	Lysistrata/The Acharnians/The Clouds
	The Wasps/The Poet and the Women/The Frogs
Aristotle	**The Athenian Constitution**
	The Ethics
	The Politics
Aristotle/Horace/	
Longinus	**Classical Literary Criticism**
Arrian	**The Campaigns of Alexander**
Saint Augustine	**City of God**
	Confessions
Boethius	**The Consolation of Philosophy**
Caesar	**The Civil War**
	The Conquest of Gaul
Catullus	**Poems**
Cicero	**The Murder Trials**
	The Nature of the Gods
	On the Good Life
	Selected Letters
	Selected Political Speeches
	Selected Works
Euripides	**Alcestis/Iphigenia in Tauris/Hippolytus/The**
	Bacchae/Ion/The Women of Troy/Helen
	Medea/Hecabe/Electra/Heracles
	Orestes/The Children of Heracles/
	Andromache/The Suppliant Woman/
	The Phoenician Women/Iphigenia in Aulis

Pliny	The Letters of the Younger Pliny
Plutarch	The Age of Alexander (Nine Greek Lives)
	The Fall of the Roman Republic (Six Lives)
	The Makers of Rome (Nine Lives)
	The Rise and Fall of Athens (Nine Greek Lives)
Polybius	The Rise of the Roman Empire
Procopius	The Secret History
Propertius	The Poems
Quintus Curtius Rufus	The History of Alexander
Sallust	The Jugurthine War and The Conspiracy of Cataline
Seneca	Four Tragedies and Octavia
	Letters from a Stoic
Sophocles	Electra/Women of Trachis/Philoctetes/Ajax
	The Theban Plays (King Oedipus/Oedipus at Colonus/Antigone)
Suetonius	The Twelve Caesars
Tacitus	The Agricola and The Germania
	The Annals of Imperial Rome
	The Histories
Terence	The Comedies (The Girl from Andros/The Self-Tormentor/The Eunuch/Phormio/The Mother-in-Law/The Brothers)
Thucydides	The History of the Peloponnesian War
Tibullus	The Poems and The Tibullan Collection
Virgil	The Aeneid
	The Eclogues
	The Georgics
Xenophon	A History of My Times
	The Persian Expedition